Advance Praise for
PhotoVoice:
Using Words and Images in Qualitative Research

"Harper and López-Robertson offer a timely and highly engaging collection of studies that demonstrate *Photovoice's* power and promise as a participatory research method and critical instructional practice capable of transforming how students, particularly those most marginalized in educational spaces, come to understand themselves as agentive knowers capable of impacting and altering the world around them. The studies serve as windows through which we witness students - from kindergartners to college freshman—deploy *Photovoice* to achieve multiple aims including pushing back on others' views of their communities, their families, and themselves by re-authoring and re-stor(y)ing those narratives with/through their own words and images."

—Michelle L. Bryan, PhD
Associate Vice President for Access and Opportunity
Associate Professor, Higher Education Leadership, College of Education
University of South Carolina

"As a teacher-educator in literacy and literature, I have long sought multimodal tools that extend beyond traditional written responses to literature. This book has demonstrated itself to be a powerful discovery, offering unique and timely resources for teaching and researching readers' responses and thought processes, with rich examples that bring its concepts to life. Each chapter provides a multimodal perspective that invites readers to explore their voices through a variety of formats, such as voice diaries and progress recordings, offering a rich alternative to conventional written reflections.

What makes this book stand out is its foci on diverse participants, showcasing how language practices from diverse cultural contexts can be integrated into the process of recording and interpreting learners' responses and reflections. The chapters also offer innovative ideas around photovoice, demonstrating how words and images can work together to communicate complex ideas. This includes exploring how these combined modalities can be used to represent different groups, communities, and settings, as well as to address community needs and social issues.

For anyone interested in the intersections of language, culture, and visual storytelling, this book is an essential and thought-provoking read. It provides a fresh and dynamic framework for engaging with literature and the lived experiences of readers, offering insights that will enhance both teaching and research in the field."

—Yoo Kyung Sung, Professor,
University of New Mexico

"In this timely edited volume, Harper and López-Robertson offer a compelling exploration of *Photovoice* as a transformative participatory research tool connecting educators, students, and communities. The book features ten research-based approaches to using *Photovoice* in a variety of contexts, from primary school through higher education. Each project addresses a unique purpose, ranging from answering questions like "Who am I?" to researching and acting on community-based issues like water pollution or political divisiveness. This holistic systems approach will appeal to a diverse group of readers from varied backgrounds such as teachers, teacher educators, researchers, community organizers, or others who recognize and wish to leverage the power of multimodality—especially photography—to interrupt deficit narratives while exploring diverse perspectives. Each chapter includes details sufficient to replicate or inspire similar work in other contexts that rehumanizes learning spaces by building much-needed bridges between schools, families, and communities through the power of photos. Overall, this volume is an innovative resource for anyone seeking to utilize photography to foster equity, voice, and connection in educational settings."

—Melissa S. Wells,
Associate Professor, University of Mary Washington

PhotoVoice

Published by Myers Education Press, LLC
P.O. Box 424
Gorham, ME 04038

Myers Education Press is an academic publisher specializing in books, e-books, and digital content in the field of education. All of our books are subjected to a rigorous peer review process and produced in compliance with the standards of the Council on Library and Information Resources.

Library of Congress Cataloging-in-Publication Data available from Library of Congress

13-digit ISBN 978-1-9755-0680-3 (paperback)
13-digit ISBN 978-1-9755-0681-0 (library networkable e-edition)
13-digit ISBN 978-1-9755-0682-7 (consumer e-edition)

Printed in the United States of America.

All first editions printed on acid-free paper that meets the American National Standards Institute Z39-48 standard.

Books published by Myers Education Press may be purchased at special quantity discount rates for groups, workshops, training organizations, and classroom usage. Please call our customer service department at 1-800-232-0223 for details.

Cover design by Teresa Lagrange

Visit us on the web at **www.myersedpress.com** to browse our complete list of titles.

PhotoVoice

Using Words and Images in Qualitative Research

EDITED BY
Rebecca G. Harper
and Julia López-Robertson

Gorham, Maine

Dedication

To educators and researchers dedicated to advancing the field of education, whose unwavering commitment to student success shapes the future. This book is for you, in the hope that it inspires innovation and collaboration in our shared mission. And to Mary Jade, whose work with families and children in literacy continues to make us so proud. Now get that dissertation done!

Table of Contents

Acknowledgments

Publishing an edited volume would not be possible without the willingness of educators to share their instructional practice and research. We would like to thank the contributing authors for sharing their impactful work that no doubt will continue to inspire and impact educators in a wide variety of fields.

Foreword

By Dr. Laura Rychly

Educators working with young people today know that their efforts must be for an ultimate purpose that is greater than the test scores that have been hanging over our heads since the passage of No Child Left Behind. Young people are as aware as ever of issues they see and hear projected into their futures such as climate change and ongoing political divisions, and the interrelatedness of the issues (i.e., progress on climate change is elusive as long as politicians are in disagreement about what it even is) can make it difficult to see resolutions on the horizon. This then further compounds the need for teachers and students to work together on what feels real.

Exacerbating possible feelings of angst and uncertainty among our nation's youth are issues related to identity when one's community experiences marginalization due to other-than white ethnicities and languages. Invitations to participate in discourse may seem nonexistent, and one's presence might seem unnecessary or even problematic. Hostility directed by politicians at immigrant communities seeps into our shared environment and can deepen feelings of not belonging or seeing oneself as a valuable member of a community. Teachers who work with Latino/a students in K-12 and college classrooms understand how important it is that the time and effort they share leads to a reversal of such internalizations. They know the potential that exists for education to lead to access of knowledge of one's value, belonging, and power to effect change. All young people today need to be full of this self-knowledge so they feel strong in the face of challenges mentioned above instead of defeated by them.

This collection of research studies is a valuable tool for teachers who recognize their work described here. Each of the 10 studies takes up a different use of the technology PhotoVoice, a tool for integrating photographs and narration, for restoring power to their students. Since its establishment in 1999, PhotoVoice has had an explicit mission to use the power of presenting images and words together to "design and deliver tailor-made participatory photography, digital storytelling, and self-advocacy projects for underrepresented or issue-affected groups" (Photovoice.org, 2024).

Particularly useful is the way the book draws together ideas across all levels of education, from elementary to college. In one study, PhotoVoice is used to help English learners practice their developing language skills while maintaining momentum toward content goals. In multiple chapters, the overarching theme of this book is exercised to make Latino/a students visible and audible to themselves and each other in ways that reclaim their identity from the margins. This is an essential first step—becoming recognizable—toward the feelings of empowerment that are required in order to know our agency and use it to enact change.

The theme of this timely and powerful book, leveraging the power of visual imagery to both bring people together and move them to action, is brought to life by caring educators who live and work each day to help young people feel powerful over what would otherwise oppress them. Accessible and practical ideas for teachers to successfully nurture their student populations must make their way into teachers' hands, and these research studies do exactly this.

Introduction to the Collection

Today's diverse classrooms offer unique opportunities for inquiry, exploration, and research that can capitalize on the knowledge and skills of our students through their active participation and engagement. Participatory research methods focus on the direct action and engagement of local priorities and needs (Cornwall & Jewkes, 1995) while creating collaborative spaces between researchers, stakeholders, and community members who often share expertise and relevant lived experience that informs and influences the issue being studied (Jagosh et al., 2012). Participatory research methods offer a number of benefits, including active engagement and inquiry that are direct products of the collaborative and shared nature of this research methodology. While there are a variety of qualitative research methods that allow for action and participation, PhotoVoice is emerging as another possibility for participatory research methods across diverse populations and in a myriad of settings.

Developed by Wang and Burris (1997), PhotoVoice is based upon the idea that words and images can be used in concert to communicate ideas regarding community needs and issues. Informed by Freire's (1973; 2000) notion of critical consciousness, which is a level of consciousness and action that can provide the potential for change at multiple societal levels, PhotoVoice enables individuals to think critically about their communities, thus prompting dialogue and reflection. It allows research participants to share their individual perspectives through the creation of visual projects, thus allowing them to actively participate in the inquiry while in the research setting. While PhotoVoice has long been utilized in a variety of educational settings, including health care settings and in community-based educational organizations, its presence in K-12 classrooms, higher education, and adjacent educational settings has been somewhat limited. In fact, it has most often been used in the health care and medical industry, with a strong presence in sociology and public health. Historically, PhotoVoice projects tend to address community and societal health issues, including access to health care, resource allocation, stories or individuals with specific health conditions, or figures in the medical and health care field (Carlson, Engebretson, & Chamberlain, 2006; Castleden, Garvin, & Huu-ay-aht

First Nation, 2008; Downey, Ireson, & Scutchfield, 2009; Lockett, Willis, & Edwards, 2005; Wang & Pies, 2004).

PhotoVoice can be used as a platform for communities to elevate their voices and concerns and transfer them into action. In addition, it offers an opportunity for communities and individuals to promote awareness and change around community-based issues and provide opportunities for action and social change. Through participatory research projects, PhotoVoice researchers document issues in their communities through photographs and textual evidence. Using these images, researchers move to create opportunities for the critique of policy and initiate change. PhotoVoice can offer spaces for researchers to investigate and respond to sensitive and complex issues while opening up opportunities for discussion and dialogue.

As literacy professors, we came to PhotoVoice with a unique perspective. Our collective theoretical orientation to literacy has strong roots in social learning theory, home literacies, and critical literacy (Bandura, 1977; Freire, 1973, 2000; Gay, 2000; Moll, Amanti, Neff, & Gonzalez, 1992; Vygotsky, 1977). Knowing that literacy and language are socially constructed, and individuals are taking part in rich literacy experiences in their homes and communities, we knew that examining the application of PhotoVoice methods in educational settings would yield great promise. Plus, because of the participatory nature of PhotoVoice, we believed that this particular method would offer additional opportunities for students to actively engage in inquiries that were both authentic and relevant to both their lives and communities.

What follows in this edited collection is a variety of examples of how Photo Voice has been utilized for engagement, agency, and action, in multiple educational settings. Each of the chapters, written by contributing authors, offers insight and reflections on how PhotoVoice was used in communities, homes, and schools for the investigation of social, cultural, political, and economic issues. Chapters in this volume provide a wide range of examples of the ways in which PhotoVoice has been implemented in a variety of educational settings for multiple purposes and goals. We've elected to organize the chapters based on the educational setting (Early Childhood, Higher Education, etc.) so that readers can easily locate chapters that are relevant to their own interests and research goals.

References

Bandura, A. (1977). *Social learning theory*. Englewood Cliffs, NJ: Prentice Hall.

Cornwall, A., & Jewkes, R. (1995). What is participatory research? *Social science & medicine, 41*(12), 1667-1676.

Carlson, E. D., Engebretson, J., & Chamberlain, R. M. (2006). Photovoice as a social process of critical consciousness. *Qualitative health research, 16*(6), 836-852.

Castleden, H., & Garvin, T. & Huu-ay-aht First Nation. (2008). Modifying Photovoice for community-based participatory Indigenous research. *Social science & medicine, 66*(6), 1393-1405.

Downey, L. H., Ireson, C. L., & Scutchfield, F. D. (2009). The use of photovoice as a method of facilitating deliberation. *Health promotion practice, 10*(3), 419-427

Freire, P. (2000). *Pedagogy of freedom*. Rowman & Littlefield.

Freire, P. (1973). By learning they can teach. *Convergence, 6*(1), 78.

Gay, Geneva. (2000). Culturally responsive teaching: theory, research, and practice. New York: Teachers College Press,

Jagosh, J., Macaulay, A. C., Pluye, P., Salsberg, J. O. N., Bush, P. L., Henderson, J. I. M., ... & Greenhalgh, T. (2012). Uncovering the benefits of participatory research: Implications of a realist review for health research and practice. *The Milbank Quarterly, 90*(2), 311-346.

Nykiforuk, C. I., Vallianatos, H., & Nieuwendyk, L. M. (2011). Photovoice as a Method for Revealing Community Perceptions of the Built and Social Environment. *International journal of qualitative methods, 10*(2), 103–124. https://doi.org/10.1177/160940691101000201

Moll, L. C., Amanti, C., Neff, D., & Gonzalez, N. (1992). Using Approach. *Theory Into Practice, 31*(2).

Vygotsky, L. S. (1977). The development of higher psychological functions. *Soviet Psychology, 15*(3), 60-73.

Wang, C. & Burris, M.A. (1997). Photovoice: Concept, methodology, and use for participatory needs assessment. *Health Education & Behavior.* Jun;24(3):369-87. doi: 10.1177/109019819702400309.

Wang, C. C., & Pies, C. A. (2004). Family, maternal, and child health through photovoice. *Maternal and child health journal*, 8, 95-102.

Chapter One

Digital Diaries of PhotoVoice:

Exploring Perceptions and Actions of Primary Students Towards Water Pollution

Emily Sein Yue Elim Hui and Sally Wan Wai Yan

Introduction

PhotoVoice, a participatory photography method, has traditionally been a valuable tool in environmental education (Derr & Simons, 2019), allowing researchers to capture and analyze participants' perceptions of ecological risks and potential solutions. Previous research has seldom delved into the younger echelons of learners, leaving a notable gap in our understanding of how elementary students comprehend and approach topics such as water pollution (Amahmid et al., 2018). As technology evolves, so does the implementation of PhotoVoice. The use of videos and sounds now complements photographs, enriching the narrative and stimulating more in-depth discussions among participants (Azzarito, 2023). While some critique the introduction of technology for potentially overshadowing the core narrative of participants' contributions, others advocate that with careful guideline development, these technological tools can indeed maintain the integrity of PhotoVoice, encouraging a fuller expression of participants' views.

The present study utilizes PhotoVoice to provide insights into how these younger students perceive the causes and consequences of water pollution. We draw upon students' direct, personal experiences with their surrounding environment. We further explore and understand the intricate connections between students' awareness of water pollution, their consequent environmental actions, and the depth of their understanding of the issue. In doing so, it contributes to the broader discussion on the efficacy of PhotoVoice and expanded digital media as tools for fostering environmental awareness and positive action amongst the younger generation.

Literature Review

Perceptions of water pollution

Research on students' views regarding water-related issues spans several dimensions, including water accessibility (Cooper & Cockerill, 2015; Johnson et al., 2015; Mahler & Barber, 2015), greywater recycling (Vedachalam & Mancl, 2010; Velasquez & Yanful, 2015), and water conservation practices. Compared to these subjects, studies on water pollution are less frequent, with a focus on effects of excessive water usage, the grasp of water pollution principles, and anthropogenic influences on water availability. While these works identify various aspects of water pollution, they seldom examine the interplay among its causes, outcomes, and solutions. There is an even smaller body of research that addresses K-12 students' perceptions on water pollution, which tends to be limited to their understanding of the water cycle and ecosystems as presented in formal education curricula (Hui, 2023).

A handful of studies consider the teaching methods related to water pollution (Österlind & Halldén, 2007; Yamin et al., 2017; Yamin et al., 2020), and others address water sanitation and hygiene in school settings (Edoror et al., 2019; Ezennia et al., 2022). Given the hypothesis that personal encounters with water pollution—such as suffering its effects or observing the degradation of water quality—can spur the search for solutions, this study probes into students' discernment of water pollution's origins, detriments, and possible interventions.

PhotoVoice

PhotoVoice is a visual research technique pioneered by Wang and Burris in 1997 to empower marginalized individuals by enabling them to document and discuss community issues through photography. Prior research suggests that visual tools can be particularly effective in capturing the perspectives of children, as they can stimulate dialogue and provide a medium for young people to convey their ideas (Thomson, 2008). While the existing literature on Photo Voice has predominantly focused on college students, preservice teachers, and novice teachers, exploring how this approach can unlock their voices and facilitate self-expression (Pan et al., 2023), there is a need for better insights into the views of younger students, especially on environmental matters.

To address this gap, the current study employs PhotoVoice to investigate elementary students' personal experiences with the causes and effects of water pollution. A multilayered approach has gained traction in PhotoVoice research, involving participants taking a series of photos and engaging in related discussions to explore the multiple meanings and insights derived from their lived experiences (Mooney et al., 2023). This intersection between technology and place is particularly relevant in the context of the current study, as students will be using digital cameras and smartphones to navigate and interact with their physical surroundings, capturing images that communicate their perspectives on water pollution (Cleland & MacLeod, 2021).

Furthermore, the study will incorporate video diaries as an extension of the PhotoVoice process, enabling participants to record changes in their perceptions and reflect on their lives through pictures, videos, and sounds (Azzarito, 2023). This approach can capture the movement and sound that may not be easily expressed through static photographs (Chrzan & Brett, 2017; Yang, 2015). While the ethical considerations of using digital tools in PhotoVoice research are often debated (Azzarito, 2023), the current study will adhere to the core principles of visual research, such as acknowledging power dynamics, informed consent, anonymity, and image manipulation (Cleland & MacLeod, 2021). By combining the traditional photo-taking approach with video diaries, this study aims to facilitate ongoing reflection and transformation of the students' experiences with water pollution.

Methods

Demographics

The study was conducted over a period of 2 months in 2022 at a local elementary school in Hong Kong. The school was specifically selected because it allows students to bring their own devices, as per its "bring your own device" (BYOD) policy, providing all students with access to personal iPads. Furthermore, the school is located next to Victoria Harbour, which is one of the most polluted waterways in Hong Kong. Victoria Harbour is a significant landmark in the city, but it is also known for its unpleasant odor due to the water pollution (*The Standard*, 2023). In this elementary school, 22 participants were randomly selected from a Grade 4 class, representing approximately one-third of the students in that grade level. The participants consisted of 12 boys and 10 girls, aged 9 to 10 years old. This specific age group was chosen to ensure the study involved a diverse sample of younger students who could provide insights into their perspectives on environmental issues, particularly water pollution, through the PhotoVoice methodology.

Data collection

Following the methodological approach outlined by Butschi & Hedderich (2021), this study employed an eight-step process using PhotoVoice as a research method, including (1) Preparation and planning, (2) PhotoVoice training, (3) Field phase: shooting, (4) Initial photo/video evaluation, (5) Group discussions, (6) Analysis and findings, (7) Presentation and utilization, and (8) Evaluation. The cycle was looped twice. The first cycle used photos as the basis of data collection and discussion (steps 3–7), whereas the second cycle used videos to replace photos as data collected and analyzed.

Photo collection

The initial 2 weeks of the study focused on students' understanding of the causes and consequences of water pollution, as well as potential mitigating measures. Participants were introduced to the research topics and were encouraged to capture photographs or retrieve pictures that depicted their local observations of water pollution (Figure 1). These visual contents, along with descriptive titles, were posted on Padlet, a digital platform, for 2 weeks.

Figure 1.1 *Layout of Padlet, the photo collection platform*

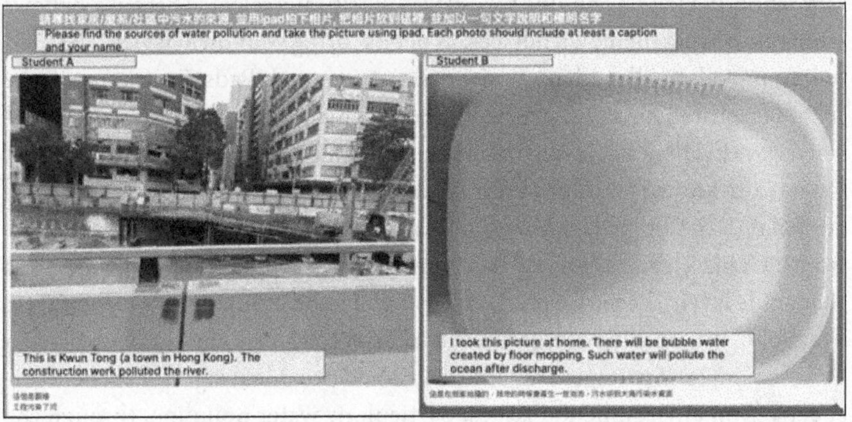

Data analysis on photos collected

The photos were then downloaded and printed out. Group interviews were conducted to discuss the participants' perceptions. The categories of water pollution sources and effects of water pollution that were identified at the beginning of the data collection were recorded as the preconceptions of taking action to improve water pollution. The group discussions on the photos from the first stage were transcribed and analyzed thematically to explore the reasons behind the identified categories.

Video collection

Next, students implemented environmentally friendly actions every day for 1 week, documenting their actions through videos, photos, and voiceovers. A semi-structured online video diary platform in FlipGrid was set up by the researchers, which students accessed using their iPads (Figure 1.2). They were provided with a set of questions corresponding to the stages of prior, during, and after the environmental action coursework (Table 1.1). Using the video recording function of their iPads, students answered these questions, showcasing their metacognitive processes and perceptions of implementing environmentally friendly actions.

Figure 1.2 *Layout of FlipGrid, the video collection platform*

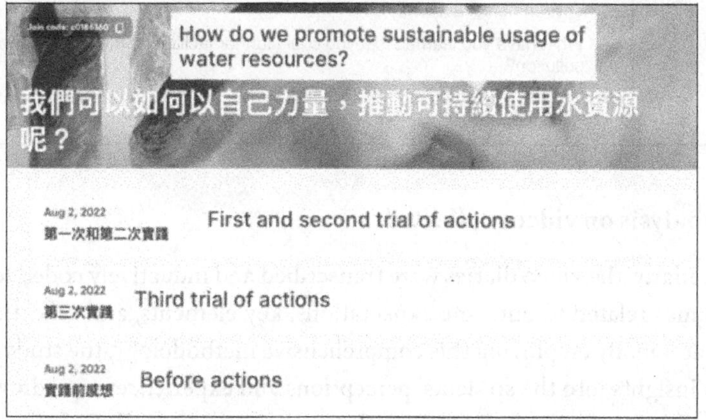

While students were implementing environmentally friendly actions, they could also watch each other's videos and engage in online discussions about each other's experiences on the online platform regarding the rationales behind the actions and the difficulties faced. After a week, students were then asked to create a video responding to specific prompts after taking action.

Table 1.1 *Guiding prompts for taking action video diaries*

Prior to taking action	1. Tell us about what environmental action that you are going to do this week. 2. What is the aim of this environmental action? 3. What do you hope to learn after completing the environmental action week? 4. Do you have any concerns about completing the environmental action week? How will you resolve these concerns?

During taking action	1. What have you been doing? 2. What were your thoughts and feelings when you were completing the environmental action? 3. Did you have any difficulties when completing the environmental action? What things have helped you to overcome the difficulties?
After taking action	1. What have you been doing over the week? 2. What were your thoughts and feelings when you were completing the environmental action? 3. What have you learned that you could further facilitate remediation on water pollution? 4. Will you continue to do this environmental action after the Environmental Action Week?

Data analysis on videos collected

Similarly, the video diaries were transcribed and inductively coded to identify themes related to outcome expectations, key elements, and reflections on taking action. By employing this comprehensive methodology, the study aimed to gain insights into the students' perceptions and experiences regarding water pollution and their efforts to address it through environmentally friendly actions.

Results

Images as a basis for conceptual discussion

The photo collecting platform collected a total of 45 images related to pollution. For the photo discussion, the students are divided into five groups. The researchers randomly assigned five pictures to the students and asked the students to categorize the photos as sources of pollution outcomes. Overall, the results consisted of 25 images depicting pollution sources and 20 illustrating pollution impacts. The 25 student participants were divided into two groups. While one group was invited to identify major themes in the photos of pollution sources, the other group was asked to name the major themes related to pollution impacts.

Perceptions of pollution sources and pollution impacts

During the group discussion session, three main themes emerged as pollution sources, while four themes were identified as pollution impacts. The three water pollution source themes were industrial sewage, trade effluent, and domestic sewage. Domestic sewage had the highest number of photos, suggesting that students frequently observed water pollution causes in their domestic environment, such as dishwashing, handwashing, mopping solutions, and leftover sauce (Figures 1.3 and 1.4). The four principal impacts of water pollution were biodiversity and ecosystems (Figure 1.5), aesthetics of the surroundings, food security, and public health and safety.

Figure 1.3 *Leftover sauce picture taken by a student*

Figure 1.4 *Handwashing photo taken by students*

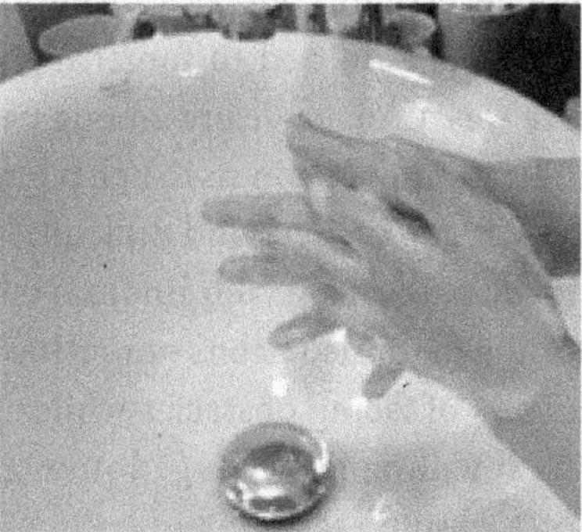

Figure 1.5 *Photo of degrading ecosystem in water as effect of water pollution taken by students*

The understanding of pollution impacts serves as a driving force for students to consider adaptive behaviors and believe in their ability to contribute to solving water pollution issues at both local and global levels. During the photo discussion, student respondents articulated a range of perceptions and attitudes toward water usage and conservation, progressing through distinct thematic levels (Table 1.2). In general, students expressed a heightened recognition of the importance of water resources. Subsequently, this led to an expressed desire to minimize water waste in an effort to contribute to the protection and advancement of planetary welfare. The students were also concerned about the impact of pollution on water resources, especially those from industrial activities. Interestingly, there was a minority of students showing a general lack of awareness regarding their water consumption habits. They believed that their use of water was adequate and did not necessitate conservation efforts.

Meanwhile, most students admitted to forgetting to turn off faucets or hoses. Despite this, there was a voiced desire among participants to improve these personal habits, indicating an openness to behavioral change. Despite the openness, the encounter with challenges and difficulties represented another significant theme that made participants refrain from taking action due to potential difficulties in altering ingrained habits or routine. There was a common fear among the respondents of facing obstacles while attempting to practice water conservation. A clear willingness emerged among students to learn and apply water conservation techniques.

Table 1.2 *Perceptions and attitudes toward water usage and conservation.*

First level themes	Second level themes	Third level themes
Individual preconceptions	Perception of water usage	• Lack of awareness about water consumption habits • Belief in adequate water usage without conservation efforts
	Personal actions and habits	• Inconsistent water conservation practices • Forgetting to turn off faucets or hoses • Desire to improve personal habits
	Environmental awareness	• Recognition of the importance of water resources • Desire to reduce water waste for the benefit of the planet • Concern about pollution and its impact on water resources
	Challenges and difficulties	• Potential difficulties in changing habits or routines • Uncertainty about how to address specific problems or situations • Fear of encountering obstacles during the practice of water conservation • Learning and self-improvement:
	Learning and self-improvement	• Willingness to learn and practice water conservation techniques • Desire to develop habits that promote sustainable water use • Motivation to educate oneself and others about the importance of water conservation

Themes of implementing the environmental action

There were 53 videos collected: 16 before taking action, 27 during taking action, and 9 at the end of taking actions. The videos totaled 4 hours 54 minutes of recording (Table 1.3). The duration of video entries ranged from 30 seconds to 4 minutes. The audio in the videos was transcribed from Chinese into English with remarks of students' behaviors in the videos. We analyzed the videos using thematic analysis. We used inductive codes to analyze the video transcripts. Three themes were identified in the first level analysis: expectations of taking action, key elements of taking action, and reflection of taking action. Then we further highlighted the sub-themes that are related to the first level theme by analyzing the same transcripts again. Outcome expectations of taking action include expectations of environmental impact, anticipated challenges and difficulties learning, and self-improvement impact on water, resources, personal accountability, and action. Key elements of taking action include water conservation actions, environmental impact, awareness, personal reflection, difficulties and solutions, and time management. Reflection of taking action include awareness of water conservation, personal growth and satisfaction, sense of responsibility, learning and knowledge, motivation, and continuation. We were aware of the frequent appearance of words found in the second level of sub-themes such as "actions," "impact," "environmental," "reflection," "difficulties," "awareness," and "responsibility." Hence, the highlighted quotes were categorized in relation to the frequent words of the second-level themes to elaborate the meanings of students' outcome expectations, key elements of taking action, and reflection of taking action.

Table 1.3 *Videos collected in the study*

Time point	Number of videos	Hours of engagement
Before the diary activity	16	1
During the diary activity	27	3
End of the activity	9	0.9
Total	53	4.9 hours

Outcome expectations

In examining outcome expectations related to water conservation before taking action, there is a notable belief among individuals that their actions can effectively reduce water waste, achieving an expectation of beneficial environmental effects from such practices (Table 1.4). The individual preconceptions of water pollution sources and effects are partly connected to expected outcomes of taking actions including foreseeing challenges and difficulties of taking action and learning and improvement of actions going to be taken. Individuals anticipate potential impediments, including uncertainties about addressing specific conservation challenges and apprehensions about failing to realize their ecological objectives. These difficulties, however, seem to fuel a resolve for learning and self-improvement, as there is a marked willingness to acquire and sharpen water conservation skills and a drive to foster both self-enlightenment and communal enlightenment on the subject. These three factors seem to be the core that connect student perceptions to action.

Taking actions

From the videos uploaded by students, when it comes to taking action, students demonstrate a strong sense of personal accountability. They recognize the importance of their consumption habits and express a genuine intention to make positive changes through measurable actions, believing that their contributions can make a noticeable difference in the health of the planet. Students engage in tangible efforts such as turning off faucets during various tasks, taking shorter showers, using efficient handwashing techniques (Figure 1.6) and limiting time when brushing teeth (Figure 1.7) to minimize unnecessary water usage. On a personal level, students report feelings of contentment and satisfaction from participating in water conservation. They appreciate how easily these practices can be incorporated into their daily routines and recognize the meaningful contribution they make to environmental protection. However, they anticipate challenges in altering ingrained habits and routines. To address these challenges, students anticipate possible solutions. They suggest strategies like setting timers (Figure 1.8) and reminders as simple yet effective tools to facilitate behavioral adjustments. Additionally, a conscious focus on time management highlights the proactive nature of their engagement, emphasizing the importance of reducing the duration of water-related activities as a key aspect of conservation.

Figure 1. 6 *Student C only turns on the water tap when washing the soap away*

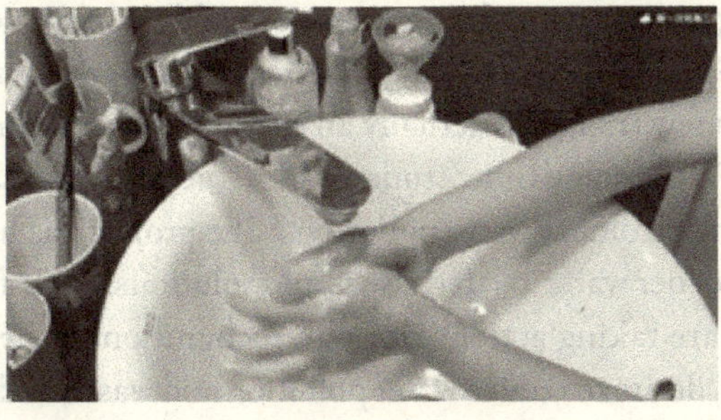

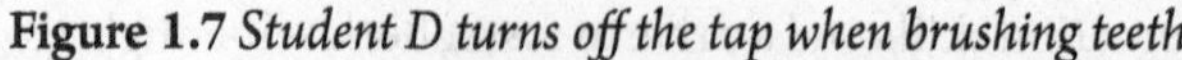

Figure 1.7 *Student D turns off the tap when brushing teeth*

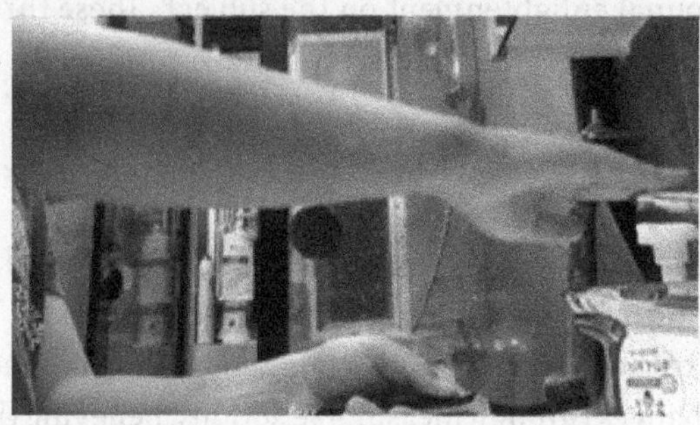

Figure 1.8 *Student E uses timer to limit the time to wash hands*

Reflection on action implementation

Individuals have come to realize the crucial role of saving water, not only within their immediate environment but also in the context of the worldwide issue of water pollution. As students initiate, implement, and reflect on the environmentally friendly actions, students are enriched with practical knowledge on water-saving techniques and more conscious of their impact on overall water consumption. Student E mentioned, "Originally I thought the action would be difficult. After a few trials, it is actually an easy job which I can continue to do in the future." At the same time, students like student F also said, "Hopefully my action can help combat water pollution." The project has heightened their awareness of broader water-related issues and solutions. Such awareness arises when students are taking actions through recognition of the importance of water resources, desire to reduce water pollution and waste, and understanding the need for sustainable water practices. While most students implemented the action in a domestic context, the awareness cultivated is needed to be extended globally at the end where students can also recognize the global impact of water pollution. Also, students developed a sense of satisfaction and achievement that acknowledges or overcomes the absence of significant difficulties and recognizes the personal contribution to environmental protection.

Table 1.4 *Thematic themes of students' outcome expectations, key elements of taking actions, and reflection of taking actions.*

First level themes	Second level themes	Third level themes
Outcome expectations of taking actions	Expectations of environmental impact	• Belief that individual actions can help reduce water waste • Expectation of positive environmental outcomes through water conservation • Desire to promote sustainable global practices
	Anticipated challenges and difficulties	• Concerns about encountering obstacles while practicing water conservation • Uncertainty about how to address specific problems or situations • Fear of failure or not achieving desired outcomes
	Learning and self-improvement	• Willingness to learn and develop water conservation skills • Expectation of personal growth and improvement in water conservation practices • Motivation to educate oneself and others about the importance of water conservation
	Impact on water resources	• Recognition of the importance of water resources • Desire to reduce water waste for the benefit of the planet • Understanding the need to value and protect water resources
	Personal accountability and action	• Taking responsibility for individual water consumption habits • Desire to make positive changes in personal water usage • Expectation of making a difference through individual actions
Key elements of taking actions	Water conservation actions	• Turning off faucets while performing various tasks • Reducing shower time to conserve water • Practicing efficient handwashing techniques

	Environmental impact awareness	• Recognition of the importance of water resources • Desire to reduce water pollution and waste • Understanding the need for sustainable water practices
	Personal reflection	• Feeling happy and satisfied with the water conservation actions • Acknowledging the absence of significant difficulties • Recognizing the personal contribution to environmental protection
	Difficulties and solutions	• Encountering challenges related to habits and routines • Finding solutions to overcome difficulties, such as setting timers or reminders • Adapting behavior to minimize unnecessary time and water usage
	Time management	• Conscious effort to reduce the time spent on water-related activities • Setting timers or using a clock to track time during tasks • Reflecting on the importance of minimizing unnecessary time and water consumption
Reflection of taking actions	Awareness of water conservation	• Understanding the importance of water conservation • Recognizing the global impact of water pollution • Realizing the need to save water resources
	Personal growth and satisfaction	• Feeling happy and proud of the water-saving actions undertaken • Sense of accomplishment in making a positive change • Recognizing the simplicity and effectiveness of the actions
	Sense of responsibility	• Understanding the value and scarcity of water resources • Feeling a personal duty to preserve and protect water • Recognizing the need for collective action in water conservation
	Learning and knowledge	• Gaining practical knowledge about water-saving techniques • Discovering the impact of small actions on water consumption • Acquiring awareness of water-related issues and solutions
	Motivation and continuation	• Determination to continue practicing water-saving actions • Recognizing the ongoing importance of conservation efforts • Expressing gratitude for the opportunity to share experiences and inspire others

Discussion

This research highlights the effectiveness of utilizing PhotoVoice and digital diaries as inclusive approaches to gathering students' perspectives on water pollution. By incorporating these methods, educators can integrate students' concerns into environmental action initiatives and enhance the efficacy of the curriculum. This also connects with Finney and Rishbeth's (2006) summary on the purposes of PhotoVoice to reach the policymakers and give voices to and empower research participants. Beyond these, this chapter claims that the empowerment and implementation of PhotoVoice are far beyond.

The learning loop facilitated by PhotoVoice formed by the connections between individual preconceptions, outcome expectations, and reflection on experiences fosters personal growth among participants. Initially, individuals hold preconceived beliefs and understandings about water pollution. Through the discussion session on PhotoVoice, students encounter other students' ideas that reinforce or challenge their preconceptions. This leads to the formation of outcome expectations, where students envision the potential challenges and corresponding solutions to implement their actions in conservation practices. Equipped with this refined understanding, individuals adjust their outcome expectations in view of future actions, leading to a more nuanced and potentially more effective approach. The dynamic interplay between preconceptions, outcome expectations, and reflection on experiences creates a continuous learning process. Each experience builds upon the last, fostering a holistic understanding of environmental issues and a stronger commitment to ongoing participation in conservation efforts.

Moreover, while the implementation of PhotoVoice is still being debated, given that trust and ethics are upheld, the multilayered expression of PhotoVoice is worthy for further empowering participants (Cleland & MacLeod, 2021). By incorporating the PhotoVoice method into this learning loop, individuals' preconceptions are brought to the forefront. PhotoVoice enables students to capture images of water pollution in their communities, bridging the gap between abstract concepts and tangible reality. Through reflection on these images and the stories behind them, students concretize their expectations for change and adjust their beliefs accordingly. The video documentation of water pollution issues not only helps students record their actions in a more convenient and immediate way, but also helps them be more reflective throughout the data collection process. As individuals progress through multiple cycles of preconception, action, and reflection, the use of PhotoVoice enhances environmental consciousness and promotes more informed engagement with water conservation. This iterative process allows students to learn from each cycle, refine their expectations, and contribute to positive change.

Conclusion

In conclusion, the PhotoVoice method, enhanced in this study by digital diaries, has proven to be an innovative and adaptable tool for engaging primary students with the complexities of water pollution. The inclusion of digital elements such as videos and sounds, alongside traditional photography, has allowed for a holistic documentation of experiences, providing a more textured and continuous exploration of students' perceptions and actions. This multilayered approach has enabled a series of photo and video engagements that encouraged in-depth discussions and reflections, offering a broad perspective on each student's learning journey. By capturing the nuances of their evolving perceptions, PhotoVoice has extended the boundaries of environmental education, fostering critical thinking and a proactive stance among young learners. The method's effectiveness is underpinned by its ability to connect with individual preconceptions, shape outcome expectations, and facilitate rich reflective experiences. The cyclical learning process inherent in PhotoVoice—beginning with preconceptions, leading to outcome-driven actions, followed by insightful reflection—has substantially deepened the students' understanding of ecological dynamics. As we observe the transformative impact of this strategy, we recognize the potential of PhotoVoice to inspire a generation that is not only aware of environmental challenges but is also equipped to address them. Also, we argue that PhotoVoice can be implemented and developed in line with the advancement of technology, fostering students' engagement and record of bodily experience for critical reflection and next-step actions.

References

Amahmid, O., El Guamri, Y., Yazidi, M., Razoki, B., Kaid Rassou, K., Rakibi, Y., Knini, G., & El Ouardi, T. (2018). Water education in school curricula: Impact on children knowledge, attitudes and behaviours towards water use. *International Research in Geographical and Environmental Education, 28*(3), 178–193. doi:10.1080/10382046.2018.1513446.

Azzarito, L. (2023). Participatory visual research for community empowerment and social change: Photovoice, Visual Diary, Photojournalism, and Fotonovela. In *Visual Methods for Social Justice in Education* (pp. 75–96). Springer International Publishing.

Butschi, C., & Hedderich, I. (2021). How to involve young children in a Photovoice project: Experiences and results. Forum Qualitative Sozialforschung / Forum: *Qualitative Social Research (FQS), 22.*

Chrzan, J., & Brett, J. A. (Eds.). (2017). *Research methods for anthropological studies of food and nutrition*. Berghahn Books. https://doi.org/10.1515/9781785333644

Cleland, J., & MacLeod, A. (2021). The visual vernacular: embracing photographs in research. *Perspectives on Medical Education, 10,* 230–237. doi:10.1007/s40037-021-00672-x.

Cooper, C., & Cockerill, K. (2015). Water quantity perceptions in Northwestern North Carolina: Comparing college student and public survey responses. *Southeastern Geographer, 55*(4), 386–399. doi:10.1353/sgo.2015.0033.

De Souza e Silva, A., & Sutko, D. M. (2011). Theorizing locative technologies through philosophies of the virtual. *Communication Theory, 21*(1), 23–42. doi:10.1111/j.1468-2885.2010.01374.x.

Derr, V., & Simons, J. (2019). A review of Photovoice applications in environment, sustainability, and conservation contexts: Is the method maintaining its emancipatory intents? *Environmental Education Research, 26*(3), 359–380. https://doi.org/10.1080/13504622.2019.1693511

Edoror, F. I., Oloruntoba, E. O., & Akinsete, S. J. (2019). Knowledge and perception of the role of water, sanitation and hygiene in containment of Ebola virus disease among secondary school students in Ibadan, Nigeria. *Journal of Water, Sanitation, and Hygiene for Development, 9*(4), 635–643. doi:10.2166/washdev.2019.132.

Ezennia, J., Schmidt, L. A., Ritchie, L., Blacker, L., McCulloch, C. E., & Patel, A. I. (2022). Water security experiences and water intake among elementary students at low income schools: A cross-sectional study. *Academic Pediatrics, 23*(1), 68–75. doi:10.1016/j.acap.2022.04.008.

Finney, N., & Rishbeth, C. (2006). Engaging with marginalized groups in public open space research: The potential collaboration and combined methods. *Planning Theory & Practice, 7*(1), 27–46.

Hui, E. S. Y. E. (2023). Integrating concept mapping of Photovoice to investigate elementary students' perceptions of water pollution in Hong Kong. *Education 3-13,* 1–11. https://doi.org/10.1080/03004279.2023.2172355

Johnson, T., Edgar, L. D., Rucker, K. J., & Haggard, B. E. (2015). Student perceptions of the Arkansas Water Resources Center, water resources, and water issues. *Natural Sciences Education, 44*(1), 136–142. doi:10.4195/nse2015.0012.

Mahler, R. L., & Barber, M. E. (2015). *University student perceptions of water resource issues and management in the Pacific Northwest, USA*. WIT Press. https://doi.org/10.2495/WRM150261.

Mitchell, C. (2015). Looking at showing: On the politics and pedagogy of exhibiting in community-based research and work with policy makers. *Educational Research for Social Change, 4*(2), 48–60.

Mooney, R., Bhui, K., & Co-Pact Project Team. (2023). Analysing multimodal data that have been collected using Photovoice as a research method. *BMJ Open, 13*(4), e068289. https://doi.org/10.1136/bmjopen-2022-068289

Österlind, K., & Halldén, O. (2007). Linking theory to practice: A case study of pupils' course work on freshwater pollution. *International Research in Geographical and Environmental Education, 16*(1), 73–89. doi:10.2167/irg207.0.

Pan, C. S., Leung, S. K. Y., & Wan, S. W. Y. (2023). Unlocking emotional aspects of kindergarten teachers' professional identity through Photovoice. *Education Sciences, 13*(4), 342. https://doi.org/10.3390/educsci13040342

Šorytė, D., & Pakalniškienė, V. (2019). Why it is important to protect the environment: Reasons given by children. *International Research in Geographical and Environmental Education, 28*(3), 228–241. https://doi.org/10.1080/10382046.2019.1582771

The Standard. (2023, May 31). *Pollutant discharge reduction works hastened to improve odor problems at Victoria Harbour*. https://www.thestandard.com.hk/breaking-news/section/4/204324/Pollutant-discharge-reduction-works-hastened-to-improve-odor-problems-at-Victoria-Harbour.

Thomson, P. (2008). Children and young people: Voices in visual research. In P. Thomson (Ed.), *Doing Visual Research with Children and Young People* (pp. 1–19). Routledge.

Vedachalam, S., & Mancl, K. M. (2010). Water resources and wastewater reuse: Perceptions of students at the Ohio State University campus. *The Ohio Journal of Science, 110*(5), 104–104. doi:10.2166/wrd.2015.126.

Velasquez, D., & Yanful, E. K. (2015). Water reuse perceptions of students, faculty and staff at Western University, Canada. *Journal of Water Reuse and Desalination, 5*(3), 344–359. doi:10.2166/wrd.2015.126.

Volpe, C. R. (2019). Digital diaries: New uses of PhotoVoice in participatory research with young people. *Children's Geographies, 17*(3), 361–370.

Wang, C., & Burris, M. A. (1997). Photovoice: Concept, methodology, and use for participatory needs assessment. *Health Education & Behavior, 24*(3), 369–387.

Yamin, Y., Permanasari, A., Redjeki, S., & Sopandi, W. (2017). Application of model project based learning on integrated science in water pollution. *Journal of Physics: Conference Series, 895*(1), 12153. doi:10.1088/1742-6596/895/1/012153.

Yamin, Y., Permanasari, A., Redjeki, S., & Sopandi, W. (2020). Implementing project-based learning to enhance creative thinking skills on water pollution topic. *JPBI (Jurnal Pendidikan Biologi Indonesia), 6*(2), 225–232. doi:10.22219/jpbi.v6i2.12202.

Yang, K.-H. (2015). Voice, authenticity and ethical challenges: The participatory dissemination of youth-generated visual data over social media. *Visual Studies, 30*(3), 309–318.

Chapter Two

PhotoVoice with Young Multilingual Learners

Rebekah List

At a Title I school in northwestern Georgia, a teacher guides a group of first graders through their brainstorming process. Her presence is calm, and she carries intention in her words. You see her sitting in a low chair, angled to write her students' ideas on an anchor chart with clear, flowing handwriting, accompanied by cute representative drawings. You hear "Vamos, mijo. That's great!" and "Ok, babes, what else are we thinking?" She encourages all to communicate: "Do you want to tell me in español, mija?" For context, "mijo" or "mija" is the blending of two words, either "mi hijo" or "mi hija," in a very familiar, caring term that translates to "my son" or "my daughter." However, this term is often used as a term of endearment from someone older to someone younger, meaning more "sweetheart," "dear," or "darling."

This teacher is Ms. Alejandra. Growing up with Mexican immigrant parents in a Spanish-speaking home, she attended schools in the northwest Georgia district where she now teaches. Her grandmother taught her to read and write in Spanish by reading the Bible and by writing letters to family members in Mexico. Though she now identifies as Latina, Hispanic, and Mexican, she admits this identity took a great amount of work to accept, love, and be proud of, much because of the negative experiences she had in school. Ms. Alejandra knew she wanted to help students who were like her—coming to school, trying to learn English, trying to find their way as young Mexican, Guatemalan, El Salvadorean, and Dominican students (and anyone else in her classroom) and her desire to encourage them to be the most brilliant versions of themselves and all aspects of their identities. Ms. Alejandra engages her students in opportunities for positive change in their lives, within the school, their families, and their community. She did not have teachers who showed her how to be proud of her language, heritage, and culture. Instead, she found ways to learn to be, as she says, "less Hispanic," to try to fit into what she felt was expected in the school culture. Since becoming a teacher, she has wanted a different experience for her students. Ms. Alejandra teaches with the intention of helping her students develop strong foundational literacy and math skills, promoting their English language acquisition and activating belief in themselves as learners, individuals, and community members. She makes learning relatable to her students and their lives, approaching their identities as assets. She sets high expectations for her students in all aspects of their school day while being loving, kind, and fun!

When thinking about ways to incorporate PhotoVoice into working with young multilingual learners (MLs), I decided to start small and work with one teacher and her class. Ms. Alejandra immediately came to mind for this collaboration as she has a unique story and lived experiences relevant to collaborating with MLs and their families. She and I began teaching on the first-grade team at our school at the same time—I was a recent transplant in my ninth year of teaching, navigating the changes after a cross-country move, and she was a first-year teacher, figuring out how to put into practice all she had learned in college. I grew up in a monolingual English-speaking home, having learned Spanish through language classes, travel, and living abroad, while she grew up in a bilingual home in the area. At the time of the research and the project, I, the researcher, had 16 years of teaching experience in different cities throughout the United States and Mexico. I taught in bilingual elementary classrooms, Spanish as a World Language in middle and high school, English language acquisition in English for Speakers of Other Languages programs in grades K-12, and as an intervention support specialist. Ms. Alejandra was in her eighth year of teaching, having taken particular interest and developed expertise in emergent literacy practices in primary grades K-2, having taught kindergarten, first, and second grades.

Ms. Alejandra and I connected and formed a collaborative professional relationship and friendship, spending countless hours discussing how to help our students succeed academically as they simultaneously acquire skills in English. We share findings, ideas, and new learning. When I came across Alim and Paris'

(2017) work with culturally sustaining pedagogy (CSP), I had to share these ideas with her. CSP promotes educational theory in practice when educators incorporate students' diverse literacy, language, and cultural practices to enhance engagement and achievement in the classroom (Alim & Paris, 2017). We found that we both believe in practices that involve relationship building and high levels of student engagement while promoting and integrating students' home languages and cultures into their learning. While our lived experiences are quite different, we learn from each other and offer ideas and feedback to best help our students. When I told her about PhotoVoice, she was immediately interested in working together to find ways to engage her first-grade class in a PhotoVoice project.

Terms

While there are other updated terms that more adequately describe the people and programs involved in English language learning in U.S. public schools, I have selected to use certain terms in this chapter because they are the terms utilized within both Georgia's Department of Education and the local school district at the time of research. The following terms include:

English Learners—Students who have qualified for ESOL services are often referred to as English Learners (ELs) or English Language Learners (ELLs) within schools and the documents that contain student data.

English for Speakers of Other Languages (ESOL)—This is the program for which students can qualify to receive support services after taking an initial screener, either in kindergarten or upon arrival to the U.S. Students will remain in the program until they test out.

Hispanic—In the state of Georgia, parents can identify their children as Hispanic or non-Hispanic in their enrollment paperwork. Hispanic refers to a person whose ancestry is from a country whose primary language is Spanish.

Multilingual Learners (MLs) —Some students from homes who speak languages other than English or in addition to English may not be in ESOL programs. At the time of enrollment, the parents or guardians may register the students as speaking, understanding, and communicating in solely English, which disqualifies them from being tested for ESOL services, whether they might benefit from the support or not. Students may also take the ESOL screener and achieve a high score that does not qualify for the program. The term multilingual learners includes students in the ESOL program, those who exit the program, and those who did not qualify, who all learn language in addition to English in their homes, families, and communities.

New to Country (NTC)—This is a term the district uses to describe students who have come to the United States within the last 12 to 18 months. NTC students can qualify for additional support and accommodations in their learning and testing. There are also some programs for NTC students after school to help support their language and content area learning needs.

What Is PhotoVoice?

PhotoVoice is a method used in qualitative educational research that incorporates participant photos and narratives to share experiences, knowledge, and understanding. PhotoVoice can be a way for students, often from groups that are underrepresented or marginalized, to create, design, share, and engage in various topics through the medium of participatory photography (PhotoVoice, 2023). PhotoVoice allows students to use photography to share aspects of their identities, their stories, and their perspectives. There is a hope that students can engage in topics that address and promote positive social change. PhotoVoice also provides an outlet for students to pose problems and think about ways to engage in steps to solve the problems, all while supporting, engaging, and empowering the local community. PhotoVoice Worldwide (2021) defines PhotoVoice as "an innovative way to reflect, talk, learn, share, and make a difference in yourself and others." There are broad possibilities with PhotoVoice to discuss, reflect, investigate, and learn about issues and then collaborate to create change in various aspects regarding the students and the issues they present. While Wang and Burris (1997) emphasize the impact of the process, including reflecting on assets and concerns from the community, critical dialogue to raise awareness and understanding of perspectives, using the photos to generate discussion, and going beyond the local community to enforce change, there are levels of this work that can be tailored to the age group and various skill levels required to complete the project.

Why Use PhotoVoice With First Graders?

Today's public schools look very different than 2 decades ago. Approximately 1 in 10 public school students in the United States qualifies as an EL or a student receiving ESOL services, which is an increase of over 25% in the last 20 years (National Center for Educational Statistics, 2022). There are even more students, over 20%, who speak languages other than English at home (National Center for Educational Statistics, 2022).

While some states, including New York, California, Texas, Arizona, Oregon, Connecticut, and Louisiana, identify students for their ESOL programs according to state initiatives, 42 states, territories, and federal agencies are members of the WIDA Consortium. WIDA works to identify and assess students and help teachers instruct and grow their students. In WIDA states, students generally get tested in kindergarten, or within the first 10 days of school when they enter from another country (WIDA, 2024). Many schools have initial enrollment paperwork that includes a Home Language Survey, which contains questions about the student's language use and preferences, along with the family's preferred language/s for communication inside their homes and with the schools. If parents and guardians select any languages other than English on the Home Language Survey, students qualify to be screened for ESOL support services. According to the U.S. Census data in 2020, teachers in U.S. public schools are disproportionately monolingual compared to the students they teach, as only about 13% of teachers speak a language other than English (U.S. Census, 2021). It can be common for teachers and their students to not share cultural and linguistic backgrounds or experiences (McKoy et al., 2017; Paris, 2016; Thomas et al., 2020).

With all the linguistically diverse students in classrooms, there are opportunities to embrace the rich language, literacies, and cultures that the students bring with them into their learning spaces. However, these students may encounter barriers that can interfere with many of their experiences in school, including their abilities to sustain academic achievement, thrive academically, and experience feeling marginalized because of their teachers' classroom practices (Andrade-Guirguis & Plotka, 2019; Liton, 2016; Rooks, 2017; Soltero-González & Gillanders, 2021). Additionally, linguistically diverse students may experience feeling alienated because what they learn does not represent their identities or experiences (Torres, 2021; Valenzuela, 1999). Thus many teachers find themselves unprepared to respond to the needs of all learners in their classrooms as the demographics of their students have become increasingly diverse (Warren, 2018). Consequently, teachers often feel they lack the knowledge, experience, understanding, or resources to meet the needs of their students (Alim & Paris, 2017; Samuels, 2018; San Pedro, 2017; Vasquez, 2021; Warren, 2018).

While there are many practices and strategies that can help teachers encourage and promote their ML students' opinions, ideas, and identities, asset-based pedagogies such as CSP can help foster wonder, creativity, curiosity, and innovation in learning (Delpit, 2008; Ravitch, 2010). With CSP practices, students can feel valued while promoting their skills development. PhotoVoice presents an opportunity aligned with CSP to value who students are, the perspectives they see, and the experiences they have. Most of the literature with PhotoVoice discusses work with older children, young adults, and adults. However, I believe that some of our youngest MLs, most emergent in both literacy and language practices in English, could also participate and benefit from the PhotoVoice experience. Throughout the process, the students will undoubtedly teach us educators a thing or two.

Getting to Know the Students

Ms. Alejandra's first-grade class was an ideal choice to do this project because she had already established strong lines of communication with families, as she looped with the class and had been their teacher in both kindergarten and first grade. In addition, the school's weekly schedule contained a time for classroom teachers to receive an extra class period to plan and collaborate with their grade level, while another support teacher would come in to cover their class. I was assigned to Ms. Alejandra's class for this planning period, so I had been working with them during that weekly class period since the beginning of the school year. The students were familiar and comfortable with me. They waved to me in the hallways, and many approached me to initiate hugs when they saw me around the building. Some would stop by my office to chat or get a sticker as they passed by on the way to get water, use the restroom, or complete an errand for their teacher.

Ms. Alejandra started the school year with a class of 20 first-grade students, but one student moved and was zoned for another school. There is still a chair at a table the students say is his seat! Of the 19 students, there are English, Spanish, and Spanish/English bilingual homes represented. Students and their families come from the Dominican Republic, El Salvador, Guatemala, Mexico, and the United States. Many students qualified to receive ESOL services at the beginning of their kindergarten year. While a little more than half of the students attended Pre-K, the rest of the students began their formal education in kindergarten. Ms. Alejandra had the opportunity to loop with this class, meaning she taught them in kindergarten and then they moved up to first grade together. Also, each student chose a pseudonym to use in the writing of this chapter: Michael, Marleny, Karoline, CeeCee, Matias, Jack, Lilly, Ronaldo, Samantha, Sandy, Jax, Sunny, Allie, Henry, Rosie, Camila, Junior, Alexandro, and Jake. Table 1 describes some characteristics of the learners in Ms. Alejandra's class.

Table 2.1 *Ms. Alejandra's Class Student Descriptors*

Gender	Home languages	Family country of origin	ESOL	Pre-K
Boys – 10	Bilingual – 4	Dominican Republic – 1	EL – 12	No – 9
Girls – 9	English – 4	El Salvador – 2	Did not qualify for ESOL (DNQ)- 3	Yes – 10
	Spanish – 11	Guatemala – 6	Not Eligible (NE) (English-only) - 4	
		Mexico – 6		
		U.S. – 4		

The Project Overview

After working together to decide how we wanted to present the ideas to the students and involve the parents, Ms. Alejandra and I came up with the idea for the project. The first graders would use photos to share about aspects of their identity, answering the research questions, "Who am I?" and "What is my identity?" They would have the opportunity to explore their voice and identity by taking photos within their home, community, and surrounding area. They would use the photos to help them tell a story of their lived experience and identity. We agreed to involve the parents and families by sending home a letter and a message on the digital communication application Ms. Alejandra used for teacher–home communication. After receiving the photos, we would print the photos and provide all the materials for the projects. We also included in the letter the benefits this type of project could provide, what to do, where to send the photos, and the ideal timeline for submitting the photos.

After the students submitted their photos, we printed off the photos and began outlining what would make sense for how the students may want to present their photos and tell a story of their identity. After a few days of working, students presented their projects. At the end of each presentation, the student presenter selected their classmates, who had questions to ask. Once all the students completed their projects and presentations, Ms. Alejandra displayed the projects in the hallway for the school to see and observe.

Sharing Ideas With Students

Before I arrived at Ms. Alejandra's class the day we began the project together, Ms. Alejandra told her students they would be getting a special visitor to talk about something new they would be doing that day. As I walked into the class, she had already projected a digital presentation I sent (see Figure 2.1). Her students sat on their Velcro, colored dots on the carpet, legs in crisscross applesauce position, ready to hear what I had to say. As I presented these slides, I periodically paused to hear students' thoughts and ideas. I used English and Spanish to explain the ideas and concepts, and then I prompted students to ask their questions in whichever language they felt more comfortable asking. For example, I began with a picture and the quote "A picture is worth a thousand words." I asked students to tell me one word in English or Spanish that they felt described something about the picture provided. We realized that just within the class, we were able to hear many different examples that we could agree all described the picture!

I next showed a slide with six images and asked the question, "If these six photos describe a person, and even if we don't know this person, what could we possibly learn about this person?" After students gave some of their answers, I asked if they identified with any of those photos from their lives and to explain. Several students were familiar with various aspects of the images and shared short stories and connections they had with the photos they saw. I showed another slide with six different images and asked the same question. This time the students were using more inferring about why they thought the person representing the photos would have chosen those photos, such as what they like, what is important to them, and how they spend their time. We discussed how the two example slides showed photos that helped explain various aspects of the two students' identities. I then explained the concept of the project to the students—how they would get to think about their lives and identities and what they value. They would take six photos and have their parents or guardians submit them digitally to Ms. Alejandra. We would get the photos printed and then the students would be able to organize the photos in a way that told a story to their classmates. They would then get the opportunity to share with the class their stories and identities through the photos they selected.

Figure 2.1 *Digital presentation to explain project*

After I finished explaining the concept of the project, answering students' questions, and checking for understanding, some students chatted about ideas and others sat silently thinking. Ms. Alejandra and I showed the students the letters that she would send home in their communication folders that afternoon. We told the students that though this was their project, we would be asking their parents to send the photos they took or selected to Ms. Alejandra through the school's digital communication platform or via email.

Communication With Parents and Families

After explaining the idea for their PhotoVoice project to the students, Ms. Alejandra sent home a letter written both in English and Spanish (see Appendix) explaining the purpose of the project and asking the parents for their help. The letter detailed how students would have the opportunity to explore their voice through a project called PhotoVoice. With the PhotoVoice project, the students would respond to the research questions "Who am I?" and "What is my identity?" The letter explained how the students would take photos within their home, community, and surrounding area and then use the photos to help them tell a story of their experience or identity. After students had taken photos and the parents or guardians submitted them to Ms. Alejandra, the teachers would get them printed to display and use for presentations about the students' findings from their research.

The timing of the project fell just before the school's spring break vacation. Several parents and families were able to submit photos before the break; however, many were not. To allow as many students to participate as possible, Ms. Alejandra and I sent home a reminder for parents to submit six photos to Ms. Alejandra through their communication app by the given date.

Class Time to Develop Projects

Shortly after sending home the reminder, more parents and families submitted photos to Ms. Alejandra. We scheduled a few class periods over a school week for students to work on their projects, in which they would arrange their photos and add any decorations, drawings, stickers, or other artifacts they chose to have a visual representation of their identity. I made an example to model for the students how to use the space on the poster with paper, drawings, stickers, and photos. I emphasized that this is how I chose to represent my identity, and all the choices were hopefully to help show who I am. Ms. Alejandra and I set materials out on a small table at the side of the classroom that students could use, including colored paper and cardstock, stickers, and foam letters and shapes. The students already had scissors, glue sticks, pencils, colored pencils, and crayons in organized containers at their desks. After I gave the students their photos and posters, they were ready to get to work! Many students shared their photos with the students at their table groups so that they could see others, get ideas, and discuss if they wanted.

Student Presentations

After a few days of working, planning, cutting, gluing, mapping placement of photos for formatting, and thinking, many of the students were ready to present their projects. I got my example out to show the students how they could stand in front of the class and hold the poster so that their classmates could see it. I also mentioned how to speak clearly and face the audience while presenting. Before the students started presenting, Ms. Alejandra and I encouraged them that this was some of the most important information they could present—their identities and what they hold closest to their hearts. For all the students, this was the first time in their academic careers that they had the opportunity to present in front of their class. Ms. Alejandra and I also explained how as attentive audience members, we can ask each presenter some questions at the end of their presentation.

When I asked for volunteers to present, several enthusiastic hands shot up. One by one, students stood in front of their classmates, friends, and teachers to share their lives through the photos. They talked about what was important to them, what mattered to them, and who they loved. Some students told stories about the memories they had from their photos. Once each student finished, the presenting student called on classmates who raised their hands to ask questions. Most students took about 3 to 5 minutes to present before answering any questions. Some students told stories about the time, place, and significance of a photo, or what they tried to represent with the photo. Some students offered greater elaboration after their classmates, Ms. Alejandra, and I asked questions. The students asked thoughtful questions about the experiences, people, and ideas each presenter shared. See Tables 2.2 to 2.6 and Figures 2.2 to 2.6 for some selected examples of students' ideas and topics students shared and the questions from their peers about their PhotoVoice project.

Table 2.2 *Karoline's photo description & student questions*

*Student with her friends *Student with her dog *Student at her birthday party, blowing out the candles on her birthday cake *Student with her extended family on vacation *Student with her gymnastics team *Student showing one of her original pieces of artwork	*What was your birthday like? *Where was that place with all your family? *How long have you been doing gymnastics? *What is your dog's name? *When do you go to church?

Figure 2.2 *Karoline's PhotoVoice*

Table 2.3 *Lilly's photo description & student questions*

*Student with her older brothers *Student with her dog *Student holding her favorite quinceañera *Student holding up a painting she made *Student holding up a poster of her favorite musical artist *Student with her dad in the downtown area of our town	*What was your dress for? *What is a quinceañera? *Why did you make that painting? *What's your dog's name? *Why is it named that?

Figure 2.3 *Lilly's PhotoVoice*

Table 2.4 *Jake's photo description & student questions*

*Student with his family: mom, dad, two younger brothers *Student on vacation with his cousins, having picnic *Student playing soccer in a game *Student at an arcade, playing with his cousins *Student at an Easter egg hunt at church *Student playing mini-golf, his favorite activity with his dad	*Do you spend a lot of time with your cousins? *What fun things did you do together? *What prize did you win?

Figure 2.4 *Jake's PhotoVoice*

Table 2.5 *Alexandro's photo description & student questions*

*Student at the jump park with parents *Student with baby brother *Student playing baseball in a game *Student riding scooter, on an outing with his family *Student with the Easter Bunny at an Easter egg hunt at church *Student at a minor league baseball game, eating nachos	*Why do you know that you like baseball? *How long have you been playing baseball? *How old is your brother? *What do you like about your brother? *Are nachos your favorite food?

Figure 2.5 *Alexandro's PhotoVoice*

Table 2.6 *Allie's photo description & student questions*

*Student with family on a special trip to Noah's Ark *Student praying for another child at church *Student in her home, wearing her favorite sun-glasses *Student with her favorite food: mole	*What are you doing in that picture? *What was your sister doing in that picture? *Where are you in that picture? *How long did it take to get there?

Figure 2.6 *Allie's PhotoVoice*

All the students who wanted to present had the opportunity. The students encouraged each other and clapped at the end of each presentation. They were attentive listeners, only really talking when expressing something like, "Me too!" or "I do that with my family!"

Student Reflections

After the students presented, I conferenced with them about the process and product of their PhotoVoice project. Since it was the first time they presented any type of work they had done, many students had strong feelings about the experience, and others felt special about sharing parts of their lives with their class. Students shared comments about engaging in the process of the project, choosing photos to represent themselves, creating a visual representation including their photos, and presenting to their class. Some student reflections about choosing their photos and sharing about themselves and their lives with their class are provided in Tables 2.7 to 2.11 and Figures 2.7 to 2.11.

Table 2.7 *Michael's reflection*

Porque mi mamá me enseñó el teléfono. Las que más me gustó son las fotos de Messi y cuando estábamos en la playa. Me siento bien de compartirlas con la clase.
(Because my mom showed me on her phone [the photos before sending]. The photos I like most are of Messi and when we were at the beach. I feel so good to have shared them with the class).

Figure 2.7

Table 2.8 *Ronaldo's reflection*

Porque quiero compartir con mis amigos como me siento y que me gusta. Poquito nervous. And they can know my family.
(Because I want to share with my friends how I feel and what I like. [I did feel] a little nervous. And they can know my family.)

Figure 2.8

Table 2.9 *Sandy's reflection*

I wanted pictures to show that were pretty. They were my favorite pictures that I ever took. Outside … in my home … another one outside. I am nervous because I have a funny picture!

Figure 2.9

Table 2.10 *Henry's reflection*

I think in my head what I want. I think about my brothers. I picked them [the photos], not my mom. I told her "take a picture of me." I feel a little scared to present.

Figure 2.10

Table 2.11 *CeeCee's reflection*

Because yo quiero una foto de mis gatos porque me quieren. They always be nice to me. I like the swing one.
(Because I want a photo with my cats because they love me. They always nice to me. I like the swing one.)

Figure 2.11

Findings

From the study, Ms. Alejandra and I discovered many interesting aspects about her students. Even though she had been teaching them for almost 2 years, she was delighted to learn some new facts, emotions, and opinions about her students from their projects. The way the students chose photos, organized their photos, and presented their photos explained how the students identified the parts of their lives and the experiences they considered most valuable and impactful. The process helped Ms. Alejandra and me understand how the students communicate, learn, and move through the world.

Choosing Photos

Some of the students expressed that they knew exactly what they wanted to incorporate into their photos, while others said they struggled to choose.

Karoline explained her process: "It wasn't really hard to pick the pictures. I kind of thought about what I have done and things I like. I made sure my birthday was in there!" Allie also had an impactful event she wanted to share when her family traveled several states away to visit a life-sized Noah's Ark: "I feel excited because I want to share with my friends about the Ark. Because the Ark was so big." Meanwhile, Alexandro shared how he had his mom help him decide, but ultimately, he chose photos where "I mostly liked all of them. Those were things of enjoyment for me. I enjoy baseball the most." Henry's mom reached out to me—she's a paraprofessional at our school—via text to ask some questions and comments about the project. She wrote, "It was hilarious because he told me right when he got home we had to go to McDonald's today because he wanted to take a picture! This is a super neat project! I think kids will love this, especially convivir con sus familias [to be together with their families]." Henry had some specific ideas and was persistent about involving his family to make his ideas happen! While the students selected photos differently, they were able to talk about why they selected each photo and what it meant to them.

Organizing Photos

Ms. Alejandra and I spoke with the students about how they could organize their photos with intention. The way they place them can highlight certain aspects of their photos, helping strengthen their ideas and experiences. Sandy told us, "I want pictures that were pretty. They were my favorite pictures that I ever took. Outside ... in my home ... another one outside." She created colorful backdrops for the photos in her organization and decoration of her project. Michael, Alexandro, Lilly, and Karoline drew images to enhance their photos. CeeCee made a border with stickers. Several other students, including Jax, Sunny, Junior, and Samantha, made their names a focus on their poster. Ms. Alejandra and I gave the students time to finish to a level where they felt prepared and excited to present.

Presenting and Sharing Photos

Understandably so, there was an overall feeling of nervousness throughout the class for their first time presenting. After they overcame their nerves, many students claimed they felt happy, excited, and good that they shared about their lives and their identities with their classmates. Alexandro mentioned, "I was nervous because I felt my voice was not going to sound right. I feel better that they know about me." Similarly, Jake confessed, "I felt scared because I was nervous." Michael was very proud of his work and he said he felt great about sharing: "Me siento bien." Similarly, Sandy commented, "I am nervous because I have a funny picture!" Also, Lilly claimed, "I felt shy because it was my family things. It was a little bit nervous but I was happy so everybody could know my pictures. My birthday, my cousins." Along the same lines, Ronaldo shared, "Porque quiero compartir con mis amigos como me siento y que me gusta. Poquito nervous. And they can know my family! (Because I want to share with my friends how I feel and what I like. A little nervous. And they can know my family!)" Many students felt a level of vulnerability, as they were sharing details about themselves and their families. After a few students had presented and they saw how engaged their classmates were and how so many students wanted to ask them questions, it was clear that the students were respectful of each other and interested in their work. Many students found similarities with their classmates, occasionally gasping, perking up by twisting their heads sideways, or whispering, "Me too!" The students were all very proud to hang their projects in the hall for the whole school to see.

Throughout schools in the United States, many teachers notice they need additional strategies to effectively reach their students' culturally and linguistically diverse needs. Engaging in asset-based practices aligned with CSP can help teachers work towards meeting their students' needs while contributing to improving outcomes, engagement, and achievement (Alim & Paris, 2017; Gay, 2002; Ladson-Billings, 1995). PhotoVoice creates a place where teachers can provide students opportunities to be culturally affirming and work towards being culturally sustaining in their classrooms.

Challenges

In the initial planning stages of this project, I set out to work with three groups: Ms. Alejandra's first-grade class, a fifth-grade class, and a group of high school students who came to mentor NTC students at this school. However, the only group that completely participated and completed the project was the first-grade class. I had a great working relationship with the fifth-grade teacher, and she was excited about the opportunity for her students when I approached her with the initial idea of the PhotoVoice project. I knew the students in this class, several of them since they were in kindergarten or first grade. I taught an ESOL support segment in the class, and I worked in the classroom throughout the school year. However, when I presented the project to the students, they were hesitant and unmotivated. They expressed that they did not like the idea of having to do the work to think about what they would take photos of and how they could incorporate those into a presentation. They gave me significant pushback, complaining about how hard it was and how they could not think of what to do, even after extensive examples and group brainstorming. This was very surprising to both the classroom teacher and to me. After the initial presentation, I tried to re-explain in another way and re-present the idea of the project, but the students met our enthusiasm with apathy or negativity. The teacher and I discussed and decided that especially with the students' state testing coming up, it may be a better use of time and energy to prepare the students for the test, instead of trying to convince them to do this project.

Though the students' behaviors in the fifth-grade class were not necessarily behaviors worthy of office referrals, the students were generally not motivated to read independently or learn information on their own. The students as a group struggled with narrative writing, especially within the fiction genre, as they often claimed they did not know what to write or how to come up with ideas. They had never done a project like this. The projects up to this point in their school career had included very specific, content-based projects that were void of their own language, culture, or identity.

Also, the students had their own school-issued devices. Earlier in the year, the media center specialist had shown the students how to use the camera on their devices to incorporate photos into documents or presentations. However, the principal decided that all devices would need to be left at school to avoid damage right before testing. This meant we had a very small timeframe that the students could take home their devices to take photos. Some students felt the pressure of having less than 1 week to take the photos and submit them and communicated that they did not have enough time to think about the photos, take the photos, and send the photos.

Later on, some students spoke with me about the project, and they actually were interested in the project, but they were scared about how they would be perceived by their classmates if they outwardly expressed their interest. The teacher and I agreed that this project could have been better suited for this class at the beginning of the school year to help build community. We could also have done some activities and mini-projects beforehand to help students think critically and utilize their original thoughts to build up the skills and confidence to be able to feel like they could do more work like this project.

Another group I attempted to work with was a group of high school students who came to work with NTC second through fifth graders. I had a positive working relationship with the teacher, as she worked to create opportunities for her students and connection for NTC students within and beyond the community. Throughout the year, the high schoolers, who had also come to the United States as NTC students, came to play games with assigned buddies, talking, playing, and encouraging them during their time in school. The elementary students looked forward to this time, as they loved and admired their high school buddies. The teacher was also very excited about this project, and we worked together to determine the logistics of the project, especially as these students were older, had more developed skills, and each had access to their phones and computers. When I explained the assignment to the high school students, they seemed excited and motivated to participate. However, we ran into some challenges. Once the state testing window began, the high school students would not be able to come to the elementary school. In addition, the school's spring break took place soon after I had explained the project. The high school students had great attitudes about the project, and many were able to take photos and create projects. Nonetheless, time was a factor. With limited access to the students, it became difficult and we were not able to execute the project the way we had hoped. The idea for the high school students was to present to their buddies and then help them do their own projects. However, unfortunately time ran out and only some of the students presented to their buddies.

Considerations

Through working with all three groups of students, I found some areas that are worth considering when attempting a project like this one. Though I found the project with the first-grade students to be a success, there are still many factors to consider in making this type of project worthwhile, inspiring, and successful. The timing of the project could have been more strategic. We started the work right before spring break, and then when the students came back, many of the classes were involved in state testing, which meant different schedules for everyone—students and teachers alike. Ms. Alejandra and I agreed that we felt this could have been a great way to start the year, and then this project could have been a springboard towards more projects and similar work throughout the school year. This project is a great opportunity for the beginning of the year because the information is based on personal identity, which cannot be wrong—it is the individual's experience and their narrative about their life. Though her students had been together the year before, some of the information they shared during these projects was new for their classmates. Ms. Alejandra and I thought that students' relationships with each other and the teacher could have become closer sooner if they had the opportunity to find commonalities earlier. In addition, this project could be a way to involve parents more throughout the year, had this been the first project of the year. The fifth-grade teacher, the high school teacher, and I all agreed that this project may have been a success had we attempted it at the beginning of the year because of timing and state testing.

Another consideration is the age of the students. I found that the younger and the older students were engaged and motivated to work on the project. The fifth-graders, however, lacked buy-in. They knew the greatest concern was the results of their state testing, and they navigated what they had to do and did not have to do to move on to middle school. From working with that group of fifth graders, I saw a significant difference in what they were willing to share with the whole group and with select small groups. Had they been able to approach this project under more selected, contained circumstances, I believe that many, though not all, would have been more willing to explore and engage in the thinking and work of the project. In the same way that the first graders asked thoughtful questions and engaged with each other to find commonalities, that same process can be intimidating for fifth-grade students. This group of fifth graders was very self-conscious and worried about their classmates' perceptions of them. Doing personal work could put them in a vulnerable place, and if not done carefully, it could cause students to retract and avoid exploring and sharing more about their languages, cultures, and communities.

A final consideration for this project is access to technology and resources. With careful planning and timing, this project could be successful even with varying amounts of access to technology. However, greater access to cameras and student skills and knowledge can affect how the students participate in the work. If the teachers do the thinking and preparation beforehand, there is a possibility this can work at any age.

Conclusion

These young students were able to participate in a PhotoVoice project where they could think about their research questions, "Who am I?" and "What is my identity?", by delving into what really makes them unique as individuals. The students chose photos to represent aspects of their identities, often relating to language, culture, and family. Students were thoughtful and intentional about choosing photos that represented important aspects of their lives, lived experiences, stories, and identities. Though it was their first time to formally present, the students overcame their nerves to share about themselves with their classmates, friends, and teachers. Students then asked each other about aspects of their photos, identities, and experiences. They learned from each other and identified affinities with one another.

Overall, Ms. Alejandra and I agreed that this project was worthwhile in helping students value their own voices and take pride in who they are. Some of the benefits of doing this project included students developing their voice, creativity, and critical thinking skills; exploring aspects of their identity and community; experiencing a fun and creative educational outlet; engaging in work that transcends language; developing agency and advocacy for themselves and their community; and taking ownership of their learning and thinking through the stages of the project. When looking back at our goal to adopt more asset-based practices to facilitate tenets of CSP into our teaching practices, we felt that this PhotoVoice project valued student voices, allowed students to use their strengths, and provided opportunities for all students to listen and contribute to the evolving mindset of being culturally affirming and sustaining within the classroom.

References

Alim, S., & Paris, D. (2017). What is culturally sustaining pedagogy and why does it matter? In D. Paris and H. S. Alim (Eds.), *Culturally sustaining pedagogies: Teaching and learning for justice in a changing world* (pp. 1–21). Teachers College Press.

Andrade-Guirguis, R., & Plotka, R. (2019). Engaging Latino families in early childhood education programs: Barriers, misconceptions and recommendations. *Dimensions of Early Childhood, 47*(2), 14–20.

Delpit, L., & Dowdy, J. K. (Eds.). (2008). *The skin that we speak: Thoughts on language and culture in the classroom*. The New Press.

Gay, G. (2002). Preparing for culturally responsive teaching. *Journal of Teacher Education, 53*(2), 106–116. https://doi.org/10.1177/0022487102053002003

Ladson-Billings, G. (1995). But that's just good teaching! The case for culturally relevant pedagogy. *Theory Into Practice, 34*(3), 159–165. https://doi.org/10.1080/00405849509543675

Liton, H. A. (2016). Harnessing the barriers that impact students' English language learning (ELL). *International Journal of Instruction, 9*(2), 91–106. http://doi.org.10.12973/iji.2016.927a

McKoy, C. L., MacLeod, R. B., Walter, J. S., & Nolker, D. B. (2017). The impact of an in-service workshop on cooperating teachers' perceptions of culturally responsive teaching. *Journal of Music Teacher Education, 26*(2), 50–63.

National Center for Education Statistics. (2022). English learner (EL) students enrolled in public elementary and secondary schools, by state: Selected years, fall 2000 through fall 2020 [Table 204.20]. In *Digest of Education Statistics*. U.S. Department of Education, Institute of Education Sciences. https://nces.ed.gov/programs/digest/d22/tables/dt22_204.20.asp

Paris, D. (2016). On educating culturally sustaining teachers. *Teaching Works*. http://www.teachingworks.org/images/files/TeachingWorks_Paris.pdf

PhotoVoice. (2023). About PhotoVoice, how PhotoVoice works and our activities. https://photovoice.org.

PhotoVoice Worldwide. (2021). What is PhotoVoice? http://phtovoiceworldwide.com

Ravitch, D. (2020). *Slaying Goliath: The passionate resistance to privatization and the fight to save America's public schools*. Vintage.

Rooks, N. (2017). *Cutting school: The ergonomics of American education*. The New Press.

Samuels, A. F. (2018). Exploring culturally responsive pedagogy: Teachers' perspectives on fostering equitable and inclusive classrooms. *SRATE*, 27(1), 22–30.

San Pedro, T. J. (2017). "This stuff interests me": Re-centering Indigenous paradigms in colonizing schooling spaces. In D. Paris and H. S. Alim (Eds.), *Culturally sustaining pedagogies: teaching and learning for justice in a changing world* (pp. 99–116). Teachers College Press.

Soltero-González, L., & Gillanders, C. (2021). Rethinking home-school partnerships: Lessons learned from Latinx parents of young children during the COVID-19 era. *Early Childhood and Education Journal*, (49), 965–976. http://doi.org/10.1007/s10643-021-01210-4

Thomas, C. L., Tancock, S. M., Zygmunt, E. M., & Sutter, N. (2020). Effects of a community-engaged teacher preparation program on the culturally relevant teaching self-efficacy of preservice teachers. *Journal of Negro Education*, 89(2), 122–135.

Torres, A. (2021) Using digital libraries to engage the whole student: Culturally sustaining pedagogies, trauma-informed classrooms, and project-based learning. *Journal of Critical Digital Librarianship*, 1(1), article 5. DOI: 10.31390/jcdl.1.1.05

U.S. Census. (2021). ACS 5-year estimates public use microdata sample. http://data.census.gov/mdat/#/search?ds=ACSPUMS5Y2021&cv=LANX&rv=OCCP&wt=PWGTP

Valenzuela, A. (1999). *Subtractive schooling: US-Mexican youth and the politics of caring.* State University of New York Press.

Vasquez, R. (2021). (Re)inscribing white cultural hegemony: The paradox of culturally relevant pedagogy? *Educational Studies*, 57(5), 509–523. https://doi.org/10.1080/00131946.2021.1945604

Wang, C., & Burris, M. A. (1997). Photovoice: Concept, methodology, and use for participatory needs assessment. *Health education & behavior*, 24(3), 369–387.

Warren, C. A. (2018). Empathy, teacher dispositions, and preparation for culturally responsive pedagogy. *Journal of Teacher Education*, 69(2), 169–183.

WIDA. (2024). WIDA assessments. https://wida.wisc.edu/assess/wida-assessments

Appendix

Parent/Family PhotoVoice Letter in English and Spanish

Dear parents and families,

We are offering the students in my class the opportunity to explore their voices through a project called PhotoVoice. With the PhotoVoice project, students will create research questions "Who am I?" and "What is my identity?" They will take photos within their home, community, and surrounding area. They will use the photos to help them tell a story of their experience or identity. After students have taken photos, we will get them printed to display and use for presentations about the students' findings from their research.

Some benefits of this work:

*Students develop their voice, creativity, and critical thinking
*Students create a research question and seek to provide photo evidence
*Students explore aspects of their identity or community
*Students experience a fun and creative outlet
*Students engage in work that transcends language
*Students have a starting point for writing prompts
*Students create agency and advocacy for themselves and their community
*Students take ownership of their learning and thinking

If you are interested in helping your student with the project, we would LOVE your help!

Please send SIX (6) photos to Ms. Alejandra through the Remind app or email Ms. Alejandra: Ms.alejandra@schoolemail.edu

Thank you so much for your support in this project!

Sincerely,

Ms. Alejandra and Dr. List

Queridos padres y tutores de familia,

Estamos ofreciendo una oportunidad educativa a los estudiantes en mi clase. Esta oportunidad se llama "PhotoVoice" y es un proyecto en que los estudiantes exploran su voz por medio de la fotografía. En este proyecto, cada estudiante creará una representación de la pregunta, "¿Quién soy yo?" y "¿Cuál es mi identidad? Ellos tomarán fotos de su hogar, su comunidad e otra área de su. Usarán las fotos para contar una historia de su experiencia e identidad. Después de tomar las fotos, las imprimimos para presentar aquí en la escuela. Los estudiantes presentarán las conclusiones y resultados de su investigación.

Algunos beneficios de este proyecto:

*Los estudiantes desarrollen su voz, su creatividad y sus habilidades de pensamiento crítico.
*Los estudiantes respondan a una pregunta de investigación para proveer evidencia fotográfica.
*Los estudiantes exploran los aspectos de su identidad y comunidad.
*Los estudiantes tienen la oportunidad de una actividad de aprendizaje divertida y creativa.
*Los estudiantes participan en un trabajo que trasciende el lenguaje.
*Los estudiantes tienen más opciones para ideas de escritura.
*Los estudiantes desarrollan agencia por su comunidad.
*Los estudiantes toman responsabilidad por su aprendizaje y proceso de pensar.

Si le interesa ayudar con este proyecto, manden seis (6) fotos a la Dr. Alejandra por el app Remind o a su correo electrónico: Ms.alejandra@schoolemail.edu

¡Gracias por su apoyo!

Sinceramente,

Ms. Alejandra y Dr. List

Chapter Three

Using Photos to Construct Youth Narratives:

"Nasty"—My Community or Me?

Deborah D. Morbitt

Middle school students sat around talking about their neighborhood as we looked at various photographs they had taken using disposable cameras and cellular phones. I worked with eight 7th grade and three 8th grade students from a Midwest urban middle school using photographs as a platform for storying and narratives. I sought to center students' experiences and perceptions of their community using the Projects in Humanizing approach (Paris & Winn, 2013), which prioritizes learning and talking *with* students to share these stories in a trusting way. Using ethnographic and PhotoVoice methods (Wang, 2006; Wang & Burris, 1997), I asked how these students mediated discussions around the photos they took of their community and neighborhoods. Engaging in a culturally sustaining pedagogical framework, I attempted to go beyond what is relevant in their lives, and as Paris (2012) stated,

> culturally sustaining requires that our pedagogies be more than responsive of or relevant to the cultural experiences and practices of young people—it requires that they support young people in sustaining the cultural and linguistic competence of their communities while simultaneously offering access to dominant cultural competence. (95)

I sought to have the students, as researchers, "assert control" over what images they chose and what they said about them (Irizarry, 2017, p. 85). Supporting student inquiry and working with preservice and practicing teachers to teach in communities often different from their own experiences, it is essential to find ways to include community, families, and knowledge outside of the academic walls. This project demonstrated how using photographs is one method to do exactly that.

Conceptual Frameworks

Culturally sustaining pedagogies

This framework is an approach that connects students' outside lives to the teaching and learning in academic spaces. Bucholtz, Casillas, & Lee's (2017) conception of culturally sustaining pedagogies (CSP) stated, "CSP fosters the full range of young people's expertise and thereby has the potential to transform schooling into a force for social justice" (p. 45). It provides a method to bring the outside in. When students see connections between school and home, their approach to learning is affected. Irizarry (2017) stated, "Culturally Sustaining Pedagogies are approaches to teaching and learning with the potential to improve academic outcomes among students, particularly those who have been underserved by schools" (p. 91). What better way to do this than having students represent their lives through images and then taking these images, talking about them, and writing what they mean to them? What are these students' concerns? What do they want to share with others? This project allowed students to discuss issues important to them. Therefore, using photos as a starting point for student's discourse about their lived experiences and community provided what San Pedro refers to as "sacred spaces."

Sacred spaces

"Sacred spaces are places within schools for students to be vocal, active, and reflective about ways to counter inequality in their communities instead of passively accepting such circumstances" (San Pedro, 2017, p. 100). Exploring a community through photographs allows students to actively participate and connect school with home, at the same time viewing their neighborhood through their own lived experiences.

> In sacred truth spaces, students are able to engage in the often-vulnerable act of telling and hearing multiple truths. As such, safety is not necessarily the goal; the goal, rather, is creating a dialogic space to share our truths and to listen *and* learn the truths of others." (San Pedro, p. 103)

The students in this project co-constructed a space for discussions around their own photographs and reason for taking them, while also engaging in discourse around each other's photos. This space was used to affirm their experiences and identities in their communities.

Counternarratives, heterotopia, and identity

Counternarratives, critical race theory, and social action (Bernal, 2002; Ladson-Billings & Tate, 1995; Yosso, 2005) helped to explain the important stories these students told. Often, discussions were not in contrast to the hegemonic views of this community. The students' conversations were complex and multileveled, indicating ideologies about positioning and identity. Using Foucault's (2008) conception of heterotopia as spaces with multiple layers of meaning or relationships to other places, students recognized hegemonic forces within their community and culture, recognized this power, and defined their community in their own way of thinking. These students used their voice to create multiple spaces and social positioning in the ways they created a unique space to talk about their community and use the photos to mediate conversation that positioned them as knowers.

How one narrates their own story of identity includes acting as author and recipient and is collectively shaped. Identity formation is how one sees themselves, as well as how they are seen by others. Students are often identified based on the community in which they live. Identity, as explained by Urrieta (2007), "is also very much about how people come to understand themselves, how they come to 'figure' who they are, through the 'worlds' that they participate in and how they relate to others within and outside of these worlds" (p. 107). How one tells a story is the way in which it is authored. The agency that is taken up by the author is in the choices of what is stated and what may be left out. Bakhtin conceived the space of authoring as individuals' answering of the world (Powell,

2017, p. 32). Using authoring, the storyteller can remake or tell an event from their perspective and from the way they view the world.

Methodology

I worked with 7th and 8th grade students at a Midwestern urban middle school located in a major metropolitan city and one of the largest public school systems in the state. Our time was limited the first year due to the lateness in the academic year (mid-late spring), but our group met as often as possible, one to two times per week. The following year, when I first saw the students from the past year, they called me "the picture lady." When asked if they wanted to continue the work, they appeared very excited and requested to take additional pictures. Three students from the original eight remained in the group. New 7th grade students had heard about the project from either prior student participants or their language arts teacher and expressed interest to participate.

The total project occurred during three academic semesters—spring, autumn, and the following spring semester—with some of the original group of students dropping out and three students continuing throughout the project duration (Appendix A). In all, we had:

- seven to eight students in 7th grade that wanted to participate and had signed forms
- three students that returned from the past spring that were now in 8th grade

Positionality

My initial positionality with the students was as a complete outsider from a local state university. Access to my site was as a participant/observer. I had previously met the teacher and was welcomed into the school due to working with her as a mentor to teacher candidates in the education program at the university I worked. This teacher allowed me to come into the class to ask for students who wanted to work on this PhotoVoice project together. Self-awareness was important for me as I grew up in this city, but not in the same community, as these students. Like the teacher in Policing and Performing Culture (Wong & Pena, 2017), I was aware that I benefited from privilege as a white, middle-class, university researcher. This sense of self was constantly examined and reflective in the work I did with these students. In addition, I could not ignore this in how their stories were interpreted and compiled for this project.

Project design

Students were given disposable cameras during the first spring and asked to photograph their everyday life. We discussed the ways to minimize potential risks while photographing. This included getting permission to photograph certain areas and/or people. We carefully reviewed the PhotoVoice protocol (Appendix B), discussing the parameters of the project, the goals, potential risks, and guidelines. Rather than telling the students what to photograph, I wanted them to take pictures of their neighborhood/community through their eyes, what spoke to them in the moment, and what they wanted to share in our group. My intentionality in this approach was to ensure the photos were not my interpretation of injustice or what I thought would have value, but rather what was meaningful to them. We met over a series of 5 weeks during the first spring semester and audio recorded our discussions. The following year we continued to meet during their 8th period in the school library. We attempted to use cellular phones this time, due to the expense of purchasing and developing the disposable cameras and reduction of waste.

Limitations

An unanticipated limitation was that often students had their cellular phones taken away at home or school, or they weren't working for various reasons. This created a challenge for all of us and the project. At times, the group didn't have any new photos to talk about or focused on why their phones were taken away rather than the project. Therefore, I shifted to use a combination of disposable cameras and cellular phones. This seemed to work better.

Additionally, the cooperating teacher was concerned for the safety of the students. Her concern was based on her opinion that these students had a lack of boundaries. According to the teacher, these students grow up in a culture of violence ("whether they admit it or not"). There are fights on school grounds among students and parent–parent conflicts that occur due to Facebook posts. The teacher had identified these students in this way and described them as "reluctant writers" in the classroom. Therefore, my goal was to allow students to use their photographs to create narratives that exemplified their own identities and how they saw the world. Primarily, taking pictures of other students and posting those was the gravest concern. At that point it hadn't occurred, but the teacher wanted to prevent it. This concern seemed mainly with the new group of students (7th graders) and not the 8th graders from last year. She said this was a different group of kids that say and do things that are not acceptable (i.e., S9 talking about intercourse in class) according to what I interpreted as the teacher's norms and what she deemed acceptable talk in the classroom. Yet, she expressed her continued support therefore and it appeared that the cooperating teacher was on board with the photo project. She not only confirmed the time and space for me to work with students but actively sought participants to be in the research project. Originally, we were having difficulty getting signed consent forms from the new students in 7th grade. Without me asking, the cooperating teacher continued reaching out to additional students, in and out of her class, and handing out consent and assent forms. She went outside of her own classes' students, in 8th period, to open the project to other students she knew. In doing so, it was her that made the project possible. The constraints and limitations with the project communicated by the teacher and the safety of the students had to be the main concern as a researcher and guest in this space.

Data Collection and Analysis

We met over a series of weeks in the school's library and audio recorded our discussions. We discussed the ways to minimize potential risks while photographing and then attempted to use cellular phones and disposable cameras to capture their community in pictures. Their eagerness to continue photographing, sharing, and talking about their images demanded we be creative. So, we had a collection of photos using various modes.

The first spring, our group met five times, after photographing, to discuss the images taken, why they took them, and what each meant to them. Over 5 weeks, these students were pulled from their last class period to participate. We then met every other week during the following fall and spring semesters during that last class period. Students each chose one to three photographs to write narratives about and include in our group discussions. Focus questions from the PhotoVoice protocol (Wang, 2006; Wang & Burris, 1997) showed:

1. What do you see here?
2. What's really happening here?
3. How does this relate to our lives?
4. Why does this situation, concern, or strength exist?
5. What can we do about it?

Field notes, student artifacts (student's photos and narratives), audio recordings, and semi-structured interviews were forms of data collection. When personal cellular phones were used, photographs were transferred onto a hard drive and non-internet lab for developing and use. Creating data logs, transcribing, coding for themes, and revisiting with students to discuss transcriptions and narratives were included in data analysis.

Findings

The middle school students, as part of their English language arts class

were presented by their teacher as enthusiastic participants but, as mentioned earlier, reluctant writers, thus positioning them in a slightly academic deficit lens. I sought to not only connect classroom and home but open a space for students to choose how they wanted to talk about themselves and their communities. As stated previously, the group of students was asked to take pictures that represented their community and use those photographs as a platform along with dialogue and narratives. They shared upsetting images and storied them as harmful environments in their neighborhoods. PhotoVoice methodology works to empower and promote a space where voices are honored and heard. It was my goal for these students to utilize their lived experiences and histories to represent themselves and their community as they viewed it. They could take pictures of whatever "spoke" to them. What strengths existed within their community, what issues concerned them, and what might they want to advocate for change?

We explored why they took a particular picture and what it said to them. I hoped to build a mutual space where they could share their stories with each other and me. As San Pedro (2017) stated, "all students have stories to tell and that the power of stories is not only in the telling, but also in having someone to hear their words" (p. 105). I argue that building this space between listening and speaking worked to develop a trusting relationship among us that fostered agency and voice for these youth. It opened the opportunity to bring their lives outside of school into the "sacred space" they were creating inside of school.

Trash and danger

The first images the students chose to photograph and discuss were predominantly pictures of trash—trash accumulating in large trash disposal containers, spilling over into the street, trash piled up on streets in front of houses, trash strewn among the sidewalks and parks, cigarette butts, and pill bottles. Because I focus on humanizing research, working with students instead of about them, I had to recognize this as an important story for them to tell. These were the issues that bothered them daily. These were the images they did not talk about in their classrooms. These were the images they faced while playing in the neighborhood, walking to and from school, and in their parks. S7 shared, "We saw that it not only makes the neighborhood look nasty" but then the reflection was put upon them as the residents of that community—"it makes all of us look nasty." The community was a representation of who they were as people, a part of their identity (Urrieta, 2007). They transferred the description of trash and their neighborhood onto themselves. As members of this community, they saw themselves through this lens that others saw. The teacher in *Socially Just, Culturally Sustaining Pedagogy for Diverse Immigrant Youth: Possibilities, Challenges, and Directions* (Lee & Walsh, 2017) recognized the need of his students to discuss economic challenges and identifying the problems faced by their community (p. 195). In doing so, this teacher was working with his students to address the concerns they had, and this is what I witnessed happening with this group of middle school students. As stated, trash was the dominant subject of the first photographs. This topic was revisited several times in our discussions and expanded to the safety of community residents when old mattresses, drug needles, pill bottles, and cigarette butts were found.

I interpreted this desire to focus on trash as very important to these students and something they wanted to address. When describing a photograph of trash

one student (S1)[1] stated,

> I have this one with this trash and I mean I know this is a little typical and could been putting this out for the trash man but um ?? how it's just all over, you can see down there ... there is some that fell on the ground and stuff.

He went on to explain that he went to his house and got trash bags, went back, and picked up stuff on the ground, the pill bottle, and some wood. I inquired into this action piece, "no one asks you to do that, why do you feel the need?" His answer, "so you don't have to see it anymore," and another student, S2, exclaimed, "so we have a clean neighborhood."

As students used words such as "nastier" and "dirtier" to describe the area, they had a value attached to this. This was a way to describe the community with attitude and relationship to their own connection to the space. S1 shared, "trash can be very harmful to children, children don't understand what to put in their mouth

and what not to put in their mouth. Kids see pills and think it's candy, pills can do very harmful things to children and their brain." He added, "this pill bottle had stuff in it (pills) and if a little kid came by and saw it and thought it was candy, that child could've died so ..."

Students engaged in discussions in our group gatherings as well as written and oral narratives around their images and would write on the back of their photos, creating logs of the pictures they took and how it made them feel. Counternarratives, critical race theory, and social action (Bernal, 2002; Ladson-Billings & Tate, 1995; Yosso, 2005) helped to explain the important stories the students told. They lived in these communities. Who better to tell the stories than them? School culture, for these students, represented a colonial, white, dominant environment structured around standardized testing and discipline as the prescribed curriculum that focused primarily on selected texts that students didn't feel they had any connection to in their own lives. The students felt they were seldom asked about their thoughts, opinions, and desires, let alone asked to represent them through images and narratives reflecting their life outside of school.

> People just throw things around the trash like other people don't have to touch it – and like he said, toddlers and other little kids like all parents don't pay attention like most parents do. It just makes your neighborhood look nasty. It makes all of us look nasty. (S7)

It is within this dialogic space the students talked openly about their photographs. Kinloch & San Pedro (2014) stated, "We have come to understand the dialogic spiral as the construction of a conversation between two or more people whereby the dialogic process of listening and speaking co-creates an area of trust between speakers – the space between" (30). During a conversation with S1 and S2, I shared, "You two seem to be listening and trying to hear each other. We get off topic, but a good conversation though." S2 then replied, "Yes, it was a good conversation." These students were invested in discussing their photos and what actions they could/should take. They not only created this space but used it to counter social justice issues in their communities.

The good things

As shared earlier, there were two groups of students, three 8th graders that returned the following school year and a new group of seven to eight students in 7th grade. The 7th grade photos were much different from the those taken by the original group. Rather than trash, their photos were of sunrises, sunsets,

and buildings. S3 stated,

> I like to take pictures of the good things. This picture tells a lot about me because I like to wake up early to look at the beautiful sunrise and I wanted to show my feelings and explain why I like to wake up early.

Students found the positive aspects of the community and connected a sunrise to how it made them feel—it was something they saw, and it made them feel good about themselves. The picture of the building

was the only one of a structure in the community that a student shared. S4 had a special connection to this place stating, "This picture is important to me because ever since I was younger, I went there once a week. My mom works there. Well, she worked there off and on all the time."

It was interesting that still another student took a picture of the sky/sun.

S5 shared, "I took it because I like the sky. Calms me down." Yet the discussions often moved from these photos back to the negative descriptions of their community. These discussions involved the violence, prostitution, and still the topic of trash. S6 shared,

> I like to take pictures of good things. There are good families in this neighborhood but then there's the drug dealers, drug addicts, or prostitutes and homeless people (counting on his fingers) along with the store around here that gets robbed every week. I want people to think it's a neighborhood, not run down and crappy and stuff like that.

This is something I continued to explore as we contrasted their photos with the discussions. Students created a "third space," where they reconsidered who they were and what they may be able to do as agents of change. It is grounded in their lived experiences and had them looking toward this as a "transformative space where the potential for an expanded form of learning and the development of new knowledge are heightened" (Gutierrez, 2008, 43). The diagram below (Figure 3.1) illustrates the concept of using the official space that exists inside the traditional classroom with the unofficial space outside the classroom, privileging student experiences, to create a third space.

Figure 3.9 *Third space*

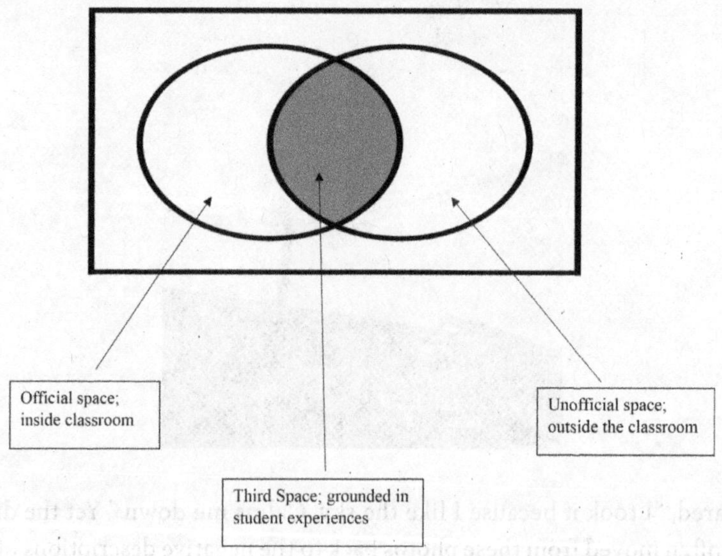

This third space was exemplified in the student's conversations as illustrated by S6 as he commented, "I want people to think it's a neighborhood not a run down and crappy and stuff." And this exchange between S1 and S2 as they discussed their photos,

S2: watch what you say around people

S1: I annoy people, should have seen last year

S2: We get along this year because we don't have classes together

In both examples, students are combining their school experiences with photos they took and how they want their identities as members of both communities (school and neighborhood) seen while building relationships with each other they may not have otherwise formed.

Implications

This project used images/photographs, taken by students, of the neighborhood in which they lived to tell their stories. In considering the theme of inquiry they represented their communities in passionate descriptions of frustration, desire, and pride. At the onset, I asked … As educators, "how can we provide spaces for young people to extend and imagine joy – to experience and theorize happiness for the sake of happiness, not happiness only as a means of relief and release from their struggles" (Wong & Pena, 2017, p. 132)? After completing this project with the students, I see that seeking out methods and places to support students in authoring of self is such a space. When teachers are tied so tightly to the curriculum, one that does not promote culturally responsive teaching, finding the places to do activities like PhotoVoice is not easy. If we look at how we can integrate this type of activity to meet learning objectives and goals, we can make those connections to students' lives outside of school.

Using photographs as a platform for students to talk about their communities and life *outside* of the classroom needs to be connected to academics and experiences *in* the classroom. Bucholtz et al. (2017) stated,

> When young people's language and culture are recognized as valid and valuable, and when young people themselves are respected as linguistic and cultural experts, then educators and students become partners in learning and in using their collective knowledge to bring about social change. (55)

Being complicit in privileging the current standardization of school curriculum creates a barrier to promote social justice activities and participatory action research with our students. Ladson-Billings shared that we could create a space for students to have agency and voice by "centering students' lives; letting students choose to investigate problems that affect them rather than teachers setting their own social justice agendas in the classroom" (WCER, 2019). Utilizing a CSP framework places the youth as experts and knowledgeable while seeking to connect their lived experiences and histories to classroom activities. "CSP fosters the full range of young people's expertise and thereby has the potential to transform schooling into a force for social justice" (Bucholtz et al., 2017, 45). A method to do this was having students represent their lives through images. Then, the authors of these photographs used the images and wrote about what they meant to them. "As culturally sustaining educators, how can we provide spaces for young people where they are not defined solely, or overwhelmingly, by their marginalization" (Wong & Pena, 2017, 132)? What were these students' concerns? What did they want to share with others?

As teachers, we ought to be engaged ourselves. Christopher Emdin "explains that students can grow disillusioned when the issues they're told to study don't tie into their life experiences. If the tools we're asking young folks to read don't signal them, it highlights a certain hypocrisy, it doesn't feel authentic" (Kirsch, 2020). As Wang (2006) shared, youth have the desire to express themselves creatively and share their lives and points of view. Although students in this project often focused on trash, there was a large sense of community pride among them. They wanted others to know it wasn't "terrible, but actually a pretty nice place."

References

Bernal, D. D. (2002). Critical race theory, Latino critical theory, and critical raced-gendered epistemologies: Recognizing students of color as holders and creators of knowledge. *Qualitative Inquiry, 8*(1), 105–126.

Bucholtz, M., Casillas, D. I., & Lee, J.S. (2017). Language and culture as sustenance. In D. Paris & H. S. Alim (Eds.), *Culturally sustaining pedagogies teaching and learning for justice in a changing world* (pp. 43–59). Teachers College Press.

Foucault, M. (2008). Of other spaces*(1967). In *Heterotopia and the City* (pp. 25–42). Routledge.

Gutierrez, K. (2008). Developing a sociocritical literacy in the third space. *Reading Research Quarterly, 43*(2), 148–164.

Irizarry, J. (2017). For us, by us: A vision for culturally sustaining pedagogies forwarded by Latinx youth. In D. Paris & H. S. Alim (Eds.), *Culturally sustaining pedagogies teaching and learning for justice in a changing world* (pp. 83–98). Teachers College Press.

Kinloch, V., & San Pedro, T. (2014). The space between listening and storying: Foundations for projects in humanization. In D. Paris & M. T. Winn (Eds.), *Humanizing research decolonizing qualitative inquiry with youth and communities* (pp. 21–42). Sage.

Kirsch, Z. (2020, June 23). *As a racial reckoning sweeps the nation, parents still await a "rallying cry" to change how race and history are taught in schools.* The 74. https://www.the74million.org/article/as-a-racial-reckoning-sweeps-the-nation-parents-still-await-a-rallying-cry-to-change-how-race-and-history-are-taught-in-schools/

Ladson-Billings, G., & Tate, W. F. (1995). Toward a critical race theory of education. *Teachers College Record, 97*(1), 47–68.

Lee, S. J. & Walsh, D. (2017). "Socially just, culturally sustaining pedagogy for diverse immigrant youth: Possibilities, challenges, and directions. In D. Paris & H. S. Alim (Eds.), *Culturally sustaining pedagogies teaching and learning for justice in a changing world* (pp. 191–206). Teachers College Press.

Paris, D. (2012). Culturally sustaining pedagogy: A needed change in stance, terminology, and practice. *Educational Researcher, 41*(3), 93–97.

Paris, D., & Winn, M. T. (Eds.). (2013). *Humanizing research: Decolonizing qualitative inquiry with youth and communities.* Sage Publications.

Powell, S. R. (2017). The self-authoring of a music educator: A journey through figured worlds. *Bulletin of the Council for Research in Music Education,* Nos. 210-211.

San Pedro, T. (2017). This stuff interests me: Re-centering Indigenous paradigms in colonizing schooling spaces. In D. Paris & H. S. Alim (Eds.), *Culturally sustaining pedagogies: Teaching and learning for justice in a changing world* (pp. 99–116). Teachers College Press.

Urrieta, L. (2007). Figured worlds and education: An introduction to the special issue. *Urban Review,* 37(2), 107–116.

Wang, C. C. (2006). Youth participation in Photovoice as a strategy for community change. *Journal of Community Practice,* 14(1/2), 147–161.

Wang, C., & Burris, M. A. (1997). Photovoice: Concept, methodology, and use for participatory needs assessment. *Health Education & Behavior,* 24(3), 369–387.

WCER. (n.d.). News. https://www.wcer.wisc.edu/news/detail/researcher-gloria-ladson-billings-on-culturally-relevant-teaching-the-role

Wong, C., & Pena, C. (2017). Policing and performing culture: Rethinking 'culture' and the role of the arts in culturally sustaining pedagogies. In D. Paris & H. S. Alim (Eds.), *Culturally sustaining pedagogies: Teaching and Learning for Justice in a Changing World* (pp. 25–41). Teachers College Press.

Yosso, T. J. (2005). Whose culture has capital? A critical race theory discussion of community cultural wealth. *Race Ethnicity and Education, 8*(1), 69–91.

Endnote

1 Pseudonyms were used throughout this research project to protect the anonymity of participants and locations.

Appendix A

Student number, self-identity, grade level, location/length (if available)

Teacher/Students	Grade level	Self-identified	Notes
Teacher	7th/8th grade English Language Arts class	White female	Does not live in school community
S1	Participated in 7th & 8th	White male	Lived in three different places; kicked out of house; lives with grandparents
S2	Participated in 7th & 8th	Biracial female	Only child, lived in my house for like 3–4 years, just me and my mom. Spends a lot of time with grandparents. Lives further away.
S3	7th	Hispanic male	Has family in other states
S4	7th	White female	Lived here my whole life; walk to school; right there in those apartments; my mom has 13 kids
S5	7th	Hispanic male	
S6	7th	White male	Lived here whole life
S7	Participated in 7th & 8th	Black female	
S8	7th	Latino male	
S9	7th	Black female	Just moved to community from other city in the state
S10	7th	White female	

Appendix B

PhotoVoice project/protocol

Introduction of PhotoVoice

- What is community to you?
- What is your reality?
- Photograph YOUR everyday life and everyday realities
    - Home
    - School
    - Community
    - Neighborhood
    - People

Minimize potential risks

- How to approach someone to take their picture?
- Should you take pictures of other people without their knowledge?
- When would you NOT want to have your picture taken?
- To whom might you wish to give photographs, and what might be the implications?

Guidelines

- Phones in school
- Emailing photographs
- Informed consent/assent

Weekly discussion of photographs and identifying themes (Wang, 2006; Wang & Burris 1997)

- What do you See here?
- What's really Happening here?
- How does this relate to Our lives?

- Why does this situation, concern, or strength exist?
- What can we Do about it?

Format to share photographs and stories

- Art show—at end of school year

CHAPTER FOUR

The Impact of Support on the Latinx Experience Around College and Career Readiness in an Urban School

Sandy G. Mason and Vera J. Lee

Introduction

LATINX STUDENTS CURRENTLY make up 25.6% of the U.S. student population and will increase to over 29% of the population in the next 6 years (De Brey & Donaldson, 2022). However, 7.9% of Latinx students drop out of high school, which suggests that educational inequities may persist for these students along with a lack of opportunities and academic supports (De Brey & Donaldson, 2022; Rumberger & Rodríguez, 2011; Solorzano and Ornelas, 2002). Understanding the needs of Latinx students is pivotal in making strides to reduce the opportunity gap for these students. Ideally, increasing the rate of high school educational completion rates and helping them to pursue higher education or a career to improve their opportunities and overcome economic challenges can be pivotal (Bowen & Bowen, 1998). In this chapter, the findings of a phenomenological study that explored how school and family support shaped Latinx students' experiences around college and career readiness in an urban high school are presented. The study sought to gain a more profound understanding of the lived experiences of Latinx students as they prepared for college and/or career paths by exploring the following questions: How have language acquisition and immigration experiences influenced the academic achievement of Latinx students in urban schools? How do families support and serve the needs of their Latinx children as they prepare for college and a career? How do urban high schools support Latinx students with college and career readiness? Several data sources were collected, including students' PhotoVoice journals and one-on-one semi-structured interviews with students and their caregivers, to gain insight into the experience of Latinx students and their college and/or career journey.

Background

The Latinx population is the largest minority population in the United States, numbering well over 56 million people with an anticipated population of 119 million by 2060 (U.S. Census Bureau, 2017). The opportunity gap that currently exists for this population represents how various factors impact Latinos, including ethnicity, race, socioeconomic classification, family, wealth, language proficiency, community collective influence, and other related conditions. It is necessary to examine how these factors affect the prosperity and educational and career aspirations of certain groups, especially those belonging to low-income, English language learners (ELL), and minority populations (Great Schools Partnership, 2013).

As most Latinx enclaves exist in high-poverty urban areas (Noguera, 2004), Latinx students often attend local urban schools, and many end up dropping out of school because of frustration, isolation, depression, or a lack of academic support (Gándara, 2008; Gilbert et al., 2017). Latinx students' academic challenges in school can be attributable to limited opportunities, access to resources, and staff with whom Latinxs can identify and from whom they can seek support (Liou & Rojas, 2016; Noguera, 2004). They often have traumatic experiences, including high levels of bullying, discrimination, mocking, and isolation (Benner, 2010; Benner & Graham, 2011), experience with language isolation, lack of connection to the class, or high mobility related to the parents' need to move for work (Benner, 2010). Latinx students, like most students, desire friendship, affection, association, and love, all of which contribute to a sense of belonging (Stein et al., 2012).

Receiving support from adults and other caregivers is an important component in the lives of Latinx students. An example of this support is related to the idea of *educación,* the life lessons that Latinx parents impart on their children and the notion that children are educated in the home by the family in addition to being educated in a traditional school setting (Arellanes et al., 2017; Valdés, 1996). The beliefs of Latinx students may also be shaped by the concept of *familismo,* in which the family is the most important influence in the life of a Latinx student (Marín & Marín, 1991). It supersedes individual needs and interests and prioritizes those of the family unit. Latinx students' families also have a considerable impact on their children's approaches, decisions, and attitudes towards college and career. Latinx families share "cultural knowledge [that] is nurtured among *familia* (kin) that carry a sense of community history, memory, and cultural intuition" (Yosso, 2005, p. 79).

In addition, beyond immediate family members, there are other influential individuals in the lives of Latinx students who have an active role in their lives. These adults could be described as fictive kin, which is "a relationship, based not on blood or marriage but rather on religious rituals or close friendship ties, that replicates many of the rights and obligations usually associated with family ties" (Ebaugh & Curry, 2000, p. 189). They provide another important layer of social influence in the life of Latinx students and immigrant communities. Moreover, Latinx students acquire "college-going familial capital" from both their immediate families and fictive kin (Carey, 2016), defined as "the rich knowledge, information, inspiration and resources students of color gain from their families (nuclear, extended, and fictive kin), transferred through lessons, values, practices and beliefs, that serve as rationale, motivation and support for securing postsecondary educational attainment" (p. 720). The notion of family in Carey's definition extends beyond biological relationships to include other important individuals in a Latinx student's life who guide and mentor them. The concepts of *familismo, educación,* and family capital informed the present study in understanding how schools and families shaped, guided, and influenced Latinx students' college and career preparation.

Theoretical Framework

This study utilized the theory of LatCrit to analyze Latinx student experiences around immigration, language acquisition, family life and influence, school community support, and resources. LatCrit expands the exploration of critical race theory (CRT), which speaks to race being socially constructed and intended to perpetuate inequality through the law, society, and economics (Curry, 2018; Morales & Delgado, 1996). CRT challenges ideologies related to the concepts of meritocracy, the existence of neutrality and objectivity as it uncovers the way people of color have their experiences shaped by racialized power relationships (Bell, 1980; Sleeter & Bernal, 2004). LatCrit extends from CRT in analyzing the relationship between race and factors such as immigration status, ethnicity, gender, class, and language (Espinoza, 1990; García, 1995; Hernández-Truyol et al., 2006; Solórzano & Bernal, 2001).

LatCrit provides a focused lens to examine the way "Latinas/os experience race, class, gender, and sexuality, while also acknowledging the Latina/o experience with issues of immigration status, language, ethnicity and culture" (Huber, 2010, p. 79). In this study, we were able to see the idea of intersectionality, as described by Crenshaw (1989), that focused on this type of marginalization as well, by drawing attention to systemic inequities that limit opportunities for minoritized individuals because of race, class, and gender. LatCrit theory illuminates these issues as they relate to the lived experiences of Latinx students and their experiences with immigration and language acquisition, as these factors impact the pathway preparation for college and career readiness, highlighting the need to create cooperative and supportive student-centered, personalized environments where students can realize their greatest potential (DeCarvalho, 1991; Huitt, 2001; Rogers & Freiberg, 1994). This approach is captured in the data gathered in this study as it related to the experiences of the participants in an urban school that was responsive to these factors.

Methods

The purpose of this study was to explore how Latinx high school students describe their experiences with the availability of targeted supports for college and career opportunities within their urban high school. This study addressed the existing gap by including the voice and experiences of the parent figure as well as the experiences of the Latinx students they support to paint a more defined picture of the supports and perceptions that currently exist in the Latinx communities that influence the college and career trajectory for these students. The research questions that guided this study were intended to provide an understanding of the unique experiences of Latinx students in an urban school. It explored the support systems that were present for both the students and the families. The research questions were intended to assist in gaining a deeper understanding of the unique experience of Latinx students as they prepare for college and/or career paths. The following research questions were investigated in this study:

1. How have language acquisition and immigration experiences influenced the academic achievement of Latinx students in one urban high school?
2. How do families support and serve the needs of their Latinx children as they prepare for college and career?
3. How do urban high schools support Latinx students with college and career readiness?
    a. What kinds of school resources and programs are available for Latinx students to prepare them for college and/or career opportunities?
    b. What kinds of community resources and programs are available for Latinx students to prepare them for college and/or career opportunities?

Participants

The study recruited a targeted sample of 10 self-identified first- and second-generation Latinx high school students ages 16 to 21. The parent, parental figure, or legal guardian of the student participants were also invited to participate in the study. The students included six graduating seniors and four juniors, six female and four male. The seven parental figures were all related (parents, aunt, or siblings) to the student participants. Of the student participants and parental figure participants, only one was born in the United States. All the participants self-identified as Latinx and emigrated from Central America, specifically either El Salvador or Guatemala (see Tables 1 and 2), apart from the one U.S.-born parental figure, whose family came from El Salvador.

Table 4.1 *Student participant demographics*

Student participants	Age	Grade	Gender	Country of origin	Years in the US	Currently employed	In-person interview	PhotoVoice journal/ Reflection interview
Ana	17	11	Female	Guatemala	6	No		✓
Mauricio	18	11	Male	El Salvador	5	No	✓	✓
Diego	18	11	Male	El Salvador	2	Yes	✓	✓
Lupita	18	12	Female	El Salvador	10	Yes		
Javier	19	12	Male	El Salvador	10	Yes	✓	
Ofelia	19	12	Female	El Salvador	10	Yes	✓	✓
Esteban	18	11	Male	El Salvador	4	Yes	✓	✓
Liliana	19	12	Female	Guatemala	5	Yes		
Evelin	18	12	Female	Guatemala	7	Yes		
Lorena	19	12	Female	Guatemala	6	Yes		✓

Table 4.2 *Parental figure participant demographics*

Parental figure participants	Age range	Gender	Fluent in English	Country of origin	Relationship to participant
Amparo	20s	Female	No	Guatemala	Sister
Enrique	30s–40s	Male	No	El Salvador	Father
Cristina	30s–40s	Female	No	El Salvador	Mother
Mercedes	40s	Female	Yes	El Salvador	Aunt
Teresa	20s	Female	Yes	Guatemala	Sister
Antonia	20s	Female	Yes	El Salvador/US	Aunt
Claudia	20s	Female	No	El Salvador	Sister

Data Sources

Multiple research methods, such as PhotoVoice, were utilized, to allow for a more creative approach to data collection and active participation. To enhance research validity, the data collection methods utilized included several data sources, such as school artifacts (Yin, 2009), one-on-one semi-structured interviews (Englander, 2012) with the student and parent participants, student participant PhotoVoice journals (Hergenrather et al., 2009; Lutrell, 2010; Wang & Burris, 1994), in addition to brief follow-up one-on-one interviews with each student participant following the completion of their PhotoVoice journals. School artifacts such as postings of calendar of activities, parental engagement opportunities in English and Spanish, and other general information that was shared with stakeholders through flyers, websites, and announcements, were collected directly from the school. The one-on-one, semi-structured virtual or in-person interviews were conducted with 10 students and 7 parental figures. The interviews featured open-ended questions (see Appendix 1) to gather in-depth information about the participants and address aspects of the guiding research questions. Six of the 10 students created PhotoVoice journals using Microsoft PowerPoint, an easily accessible digital presentation app, and were asked to complete journal prompts with student-selected pictures, intended to capture important aspects of their home life and school. The journal prompts encouraged students to capture images regarding their journey, influences, and inspirations towards college and career pursuits. This allowed the students to paint a clear picture of their experience, as a supplemental data source, to bring to life their responses and serve as an illustrative complement to the students' one-on-one interviews.

The journal prompt questions included:

1. What are the things that, as a Latinx student, bring you the most pride and represent you as a soon-to-be graduate?
2. What are the things around you that inspire you to graduate?
3. Who are the people in your life that support your educational journey?
4. What are the things that represent your biggest support for graduation, your college, and your career pursuits?

5. What are the things that remind you of your journey as a Latinx student in school?

According to Lutrell (2010), participants who can provide pictures of the environment, expressions, and moments that tell a story with inclusive details are able to communicate their viewpoints and their "funds of knowledge" (p. 226).

The use of these multi-modality PhotoVoice journals (Hergenrather et al., 2009; Lutrell, 2010; Wang & Burris, 1994) also provided students with opportunities for increased reflection of their lived experiences and gave voice to those who are often underrepresented. The use of e-tools allowed for a focus on authenticity, explicitness, integration, and critical thinking (Parkes et al., 2013; Parkes & Kajder, 2010). The use of the PhotoVoice journals can help to change people's perceptions once they involve themselves in the process of capturing images to tell their story. The participants can become storytellers and use their photographs to connect with those who are learning their story and are able to make connections to and affirm their experiences (Wang & Burris, 1994).

In addition, there were six follow-up interviews with students who completed PhotoVoice journals. The interviews featured open-ended questions to gather in-depth information about the participants and address aspects of the guiding research questions. However, not all student participants were able to complete the journals due to limited technology access at the time of the study. Only the students that completed PhotoVoice journals participated in the follow-up interviews.

Data Analysis

The data were analyzed, coded, and categorized as themes emerged after thorough review of the transcripts after two cycles of coding, using descriptive codes that allowed the most flexibility for creating categories using ATLAS.ti. The use of triangulation techniques identified by the coding processes used by Saldaña (2009) allowed for identifying common trends in collected data. Various codes were developed and sorted for easy identification during the selection of high-frequency codes. Theming the data (Saldaña, 2009) helped to identify emergent themes (Table 4.3) that developed from the categories that originally stemmed from the axial codes.

Table 4.3 *High frequency categories and count*

Categories	Frequency
Support	68
Education	53
Uncertainty	43
Family support	36
Language barrier	29
Family	26
Motivation	24
Gratitude	23
Immigration	18
Challenges	18

Table 4.4 *Student participants: Theme and sub-theme frequency*

Theme and subheme frequency for students	Ana	Mauricio	Diego	Lupita	Javier	Ofelia	Esteban	Liliana	Evelin	Lorena	Totals
Support of the whole child	2	9	6	4	14	2	15	19	6	7	**84**
•academics	7	3		4		5	8	2	3	5	37
•college and career pathways	4		9	3		2		3	4		25
•social/familial	6	2	3	9	3	5		5	3		36
Traversing language access	6	9	3	6	9	4	13	4		4	**58**
•encountering obstacles as an immigrant	9	4		5		2	4		5	2	31
•language learning	7		7	2	5		6			9	36
The challenges of the American Dream	3	5	10	6	3	8	2	6	7	2	**52**
•acculturation	9		6		3	5		2	5		30
•real world transition	3		4	5		6		7			25
•emotional self-awareness	1	2	5		8		6		3	5	30
CODE TOTAL											**444**

Table 4.5 *Parental figure participants: Theme and sub-theme frequency*

Theme and subtheme frequency for parent figures	Amparo	Enrique	Cristina	Mercedes	Teresa	Antonia	Claudia	Totals
Support of the whole child	3	2	3	4	9	13	8	**42**
•academics			3	2	4	2		11
•college and career pathways	5	4		3		2	2	16
•social/familial	3	1	3		5		6	18
Traversing language access	6		8	2	8	5	7	**36**
•encountering obstacles as an immigrant	1	5		3		2	4	15
•language learning			5		7			12
The challenges of the American Dream	2	3		7	6	3	9	**30**
•acculturation	3	3		4	4		6	20
•real world transition			6			7	2	15
•emotional self-awareness		5	5		2	3	6	21
CODE TOTAL								**236**

Findings

College and career readiness is directly correlated to academic success, and it is important to understand the opportunity gaps that exist for Latinx students (Gonzalez et al., 2012). There were three predominant themes that were found across the PhotoVoice journal and interview data (see Figure 4.1) that revealed what the experiences of Latinx students were around college and career readiness and how they were supported with specific resources and services both inside and outside of school.

Figure 4.1 *Themes and sub-themes from second-cycle coding*

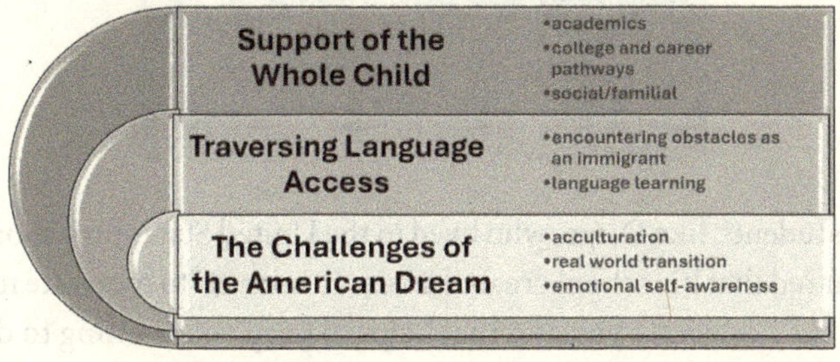

The first theme, "Supporting the Whole Child," referred to support for the student or the student's family, including academic, wellness, college, and career readiness resources. The findings demonstrated how the school presents opportunities, such as college application and financial aid workshops for students and families, campus and facility tours for college and career interests, guest speakers, food distribution, direct service provider references, and mental health services for students and families. These collective opportunities, supports, and resources are some of the elements that were highlighted by the participants as part of their experience as Latinx students in preparation for college and career readiness in an urban high school.

Utilizing PhotoVoice journals allowed the students to convey the things they were most proud of as a soon-to-be graduate, and one participant, Ana, proudly displayed her collection of honor roll medals (Image 1) in her PhotoVoice journal. She stated that they keep her motivated to continue achieving academic milestones each semester. Ana had relied on her school for educational support and guidance, acknowledging that she needed motivation to stay on course as a student. She shared that she liked being back in person to learn, since her first 2 years in high school were completed through online classes due to COVID-19. She said her school could now do things like celebrate in person, which she felt was important for students "to feel happy about school and their education."

Image 1 *Ana's honor roll medals*

Other students, like Diego, who lived in the United States for a short amount of time, shared that his school created an environment "to motivate me to keep going and they celebrate you and that helps to keep you wanting to do better."

Diego shared pictures of items that kept him driven in his PhotoVoice journal (see Images 2, 3, and 4). The first picture is an inspirational graduation display in school. The second picture is of Diego's aunt, who worked in the school that he attended as she provided support to him throughout his educational journey. During an interview with Diego he shared that his mother died and he arrived in the United States to live with his aunt, who adopted him. The third picture Diego shared is of his award certificates, including awards for perfect attendance, honor roll and athletic award recognition, and his medal for exiting his ESOL classes after enrolling in his school 2 years ago. He also worked hard with his teachers after school, all of whom contributed to his success (Image 5). It is through the use of PhotoVoice that students were able to share personal artifacts of the people, places, and events that were meaningful and important to their college and career aspirations.

Image 2 *School display in the hallway*

Image 3 *Diego's aunt, who adopted him when his mother died*

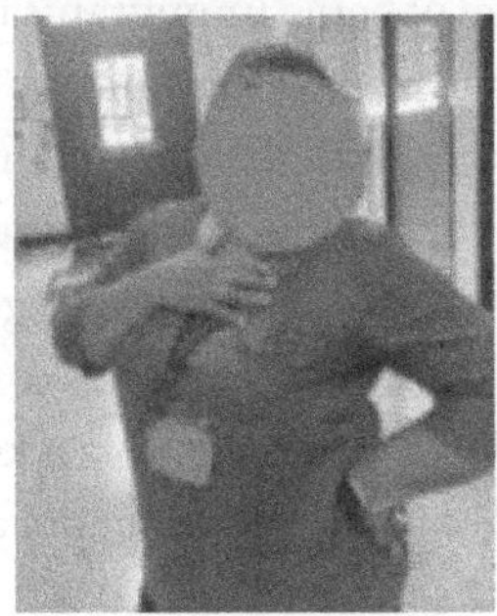

Image 4 *Diego's awards*

Image 5 *Diego's teacher*

The second theme, "Traversing Language Access," describes the challenges that the students experienced of being immigrants in the United States, including trying to navigate college and career options without knowing English. They referenced the challenges of being immigrants in the United States and trying to navigate without knowing English (there was one exception as one student did immigrate with scholarly fluency in English). Students and their parental figures discussed how this impacted access to education, health, wellness, and college and career options. Language was a key part of the participant's experience as a Latinx student in their high school as they prepared for college and career opportunities, and it presented challenges to them as they navigated various systems without knowing the English language.

Using PhotoVoice journals provided a chance for the researcher to unpack and connect with the student participants who were able to share their experiences and lend an additional voice to their experiences as it connected to issues around language. For instance, Lorena is a student who struggled in school when she first arrived in the United States as a middle school student. She found that only a few teachers spoke Spanish and understood how frustrated she felt not having friends and not speaking English. She shared a picture of herself and the social support group she belonged to at her school (see Image 6). Some of those same members were also her fellow college preparatory group members who worked with an outside agency to prepare for college, write essays, learn soft skills, and develop leadership skills; they are pictured in Image 7. Lorena shared these pictures in response to the PhotoVoice journal prompt that asked her to share images of the things that inspire her to graduate and brought her the most pride as a graduation candidate. Lorena, who struggled academically before arriving at her high school, in part due to language challenges, became an honor roll student and scholar-athlete and earned a full scholarship to college. Lorena is pictured with the founding principal of the school as she received her principal honor roll award. Lorena was the valedictorian of her class (Image 8). She shared her class rings and tassels (Image 9), earned during her educational journey in the United States as she prepared for graduation.

Image 6 *Lorena's social support group*

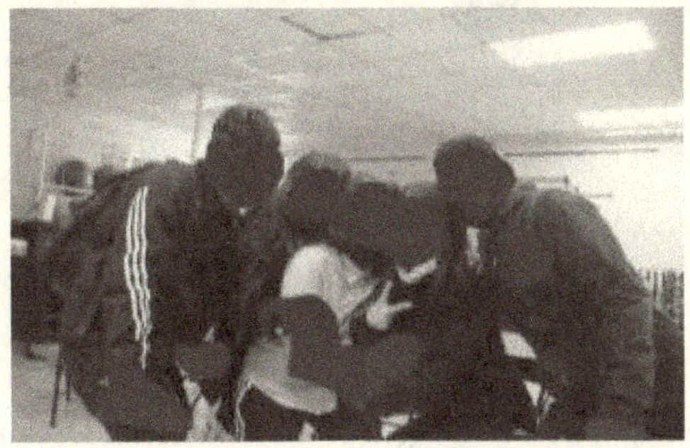

Image 7 *Lorena's college readiness group*

Image 8 *Lorena's principal honor roll award*

Image 9 *Lorena's tassels and rings from middle and high school graduations*

The third theme, "The Challenges of the American Dream," related to the many cultural adjustments the students and their families needed to make to adapt to living in the United States. The data revealed the many cultural adjustments the participants had to incorporate into the way they approached life in the country they adopted as their new home. This theme explores the many unexpected shifts in perspective, behavior, and beliefs that occur when they are faced with these unknown challenges. All the female students shared that they had been bullied when they first arrived in the United States because they did not speak English. Ofelia, a student from El Salvador, said that when she was in elementary school, her bullying experience was the worst. She shared, "I used to get bullied because I did not know any English or anything. So, the word they would call me was *hija*. That is another rude word for saying non-speaking English and stuff." Ofelia talked about the many obstacles related to the unknown encountered by her family when they first arrived, without documents, papers, licenses, or a car. No one in her family knew any English and they could not navigate the process to enroll her in school. They also were met with obstacles with navigating transportation, so they had to walk everywhere. Ofelia commented about the weather and how ill-equipped her family was, especially for her first winter at the age of 9, without coats and socks. Ofelia shared pictures of her family (Image 10) and of the friends (Image 11 and 12) that she made during her academic journey with whom she shared similar life journeys and that she plans on keeping for the rest of her life.

Image 10 *Ofelia's family*

Image 11 *Ofelia's friends*

Image 12 *Ofelia's friends at graduation*

Discussion

The findings from this study illuminated the individual and collective experiences of Latinx students as they transitioned from high school to postsecondary or vocational opportunities. Community and school resources played a vital role in supporting Latinx high school students as they end their matriculation and prepare for continued education or work following graduation. The participants mentioned that their school addressed their needs in a way that was customized and accessible to them and to their families by aligning community resources that assisted with immigration matters, health and wellness, college access programs, career exposure, various workshops for families, and programming that supported student growth and confidence. These services added to the level of support that the families needed to overcome some of the obstacles they experienced by lowering family stress, increasing parental engagement, and reducing chronic absenteeism. The students and parents spoke very highly of their school and considered the school and staff as part of their communities, along with their own family members.

Familial and social support was an integral part of the decision-making process for the Latinx high school students. Reese et al. (1995) made the distinction that *educación* refers to the life lessons that Latinx parental figures impart to their relatives. Many of the students mentioned the motivation and advice that their parental figures shared with them regarding hard work, focus, time management, and the choosing of friends. The concept of "college-going familial capital" as defined by Carey (2016) speaks to the inspiration and knowledge passed along from family and friends that provide motivation and encouragement to students who aspire to attend college. Many will not go away to college, as it would mean leaving their families, and this separation can trigger conflict and stress for Latinx parents and students that other ethnicities and races may not face (Turcios-Cotto & Milan, 2013). In addition, some of the students' undocumented status was a barrier for them in receiving federal financial aid, because they are not qualified to receive federal student loans or grants that would enable them to afford college.

Latinx students in this study experienced major challenges related to immigration and language acquisition. Many of the students discussed the bullying, neglect, and isolation they experienced at school, which produced trauma for them as students (Benner, 2010; Benner & Graham, 2011). Entering high school was a transformative experience for these students. The high school created a cooperative and supportive student-centered, personalized environment that the students needed (DeCarvalho, 1991; Huitt, 2001; Rogers & Freiberg, 1994). This model was created by the founding principal, who was himself a newcomer to the country as a child. He envisioned a place where the students could feel like a part of a greater community of family and support. The current school model, operating as a true community school, proactively addressed many of the needs that a first- or second-generation student (and family) would experience while remaining focused on what students needed to thrive and be successful. Many of the students shared their experiences with other groups at their school or with staff that helped them overcome their feelings of isolation. The PhotoVoice journals and interviews captured the transformative effects of the nurturing and caring environment that the high school provided, in which the teachers became a major source of support. Many of the students experienced acculturative stress and discussed the challenges their parents and families encountered when they first arrived in the United States, such as the lack of access to transportation or employment due to language barriers. Their high school ensured that they had mental health services, guidance counselors, and community agencies that provided aid and support to help them overcome their challenges.

Conclusion

Latinx students depend on the support provided by the school and community, as well as those of their family and friends, in preparation for college and career. There were several important takeaways that were derived from the study. First, linguistic challenges and immigration issues influenced the students' language acquisition and immigration experiences, which affected their academic achievement in school. These experiences consisted of negative experiences with bullying and isolation but also positive experiences within a caring high school culture. Second, the families served the needs of their Latinx children as they prepared for college and careers through emotional and motivational support that included life advice. The concept of *familismo* referred to the extended family of the school, as it became part of the community of support for the students. Third, the assistance and resources provided by the school included not only academic assistance around language needs and general information about college and career readiness, but also social support, leadership development, and wraparound services for students and families. Finally, the use of PhotoVoice journals helped to capture the vivid importance of the families, friends, and achievements in illustrating the value of these individuals and events in the lives of the students.

References

Arellanes, J. A., Viramontez Anguiano, R. P., & Lohman, B. J. (2017). The desire to thrive: Families overcoming economic hardships through educational aspirations. *Journal of Family and Economic Issues, 38*(3), 338–353. https://dx.doi.org.ezproxy2.library.drexel.edu/10.1007/s10834-017-9539-2

Bell, D. (1980). *Race, racism, and American law*. Little, Brown & Co.

Benner, A. D. (2010). Latino adolescents' loneliness, academic performance, and the buffering nature of friendships. *Journal of Youth and Adolescence, 40*(5), 556–567. https://doi:10.1007/s10964-010-9561-2

Benner, A. D., & Graham, S. (2011). Latino adolescents' experiences of discrimination across the first 2 years of high school: Correlates and influences on educational outcomes. *Child Development, 82*(2), 508–519. https://doi:10.1111/j.1467-8624.2010.01524.x

Bowen, G. L., & Bowen, N. K. (1998). The mediating role of educational meaning in the relationship between home academic culture and academic performance. *Family Relations: Interdisciplinary Journal of Applied Family Studies, 47*, 45–51. https://doi.org/10.2307/584850

Carey, R. L. (2016). "Keep that in mind ... You're gonna go to college": Family influence on the college going processes of Black and Latino high school boys. *The Urban Review, 48*(5), 718–742. https://doi:10.1007/s11256-016-0375-8

Crenshaw, K. (1989). Demarginalizing the intersection of race and sex: A black feminist critique of antidiscrimination doctrine. In K. Maschke (Ed.), *Feminist Legal Theories* (pp. 139–168). Routledge.

Curry, T. (2018). Critical race theory. *Britannica*. https://www.britannica.com/topic/critical-race-theory

De Brey, C., & Donaldson, K. (2022). *National Center for Education Statistics (NCES) home page, part of the U.S. Department of Education*. National Center for Education Statistics (NCES) Home Page, a part of the U.S. Department of Education. https://nces.ed.gov/

DeCarvalho, R. (1991). The humanistic paradigm in education. *The Humanistic Psychologist, 19*(1), 88–104. https://doi.org/10.1080/08873267.1991.9986754

Ebaugh, H. R., & Curry, M. (2000). Fictive kin as social capital in new immigrant communities. *Sociological Perspectives, 43*(2), 189–209. https://doi.org/10.2307/1389793

Englander, M. (2012). The interview: Data collection in descriptive phenomenological human scientific research. *Journal of Phenomenological Psychology, 43*(1), 13–35. https://doi:10.1163/156916212x632943

Espinoza, L. (1990). Masks and other disguises: Exposing legal Academia. *Harvard Law Review*, 103, 1878–1886.

Gándara, P. (2008). The crisis in the education of Latino students. https://www.nea.org/home/17404.htm

Garcia, R. (1995). Critical race theory and Proposition 187: The racial politics of immigration law. *Chicano-Latino Law Review*, 17, 118-148.

Gilbert, L. R., Brown, C. S., & Mistry, R. S. (2017). Latino immigrant parents' financial stress, depression, and academic involvement predicting child academic success. *Psychology in the Schools*, 54(9), 1202–1215. https://doi:10.1002/pits.22067

González, L. M., Stein, G. L., & Huq, N. (2012). The influence of cultural identity and perceived barriers on college-going beliefs and aspirations of Latino youth in emerging immigrant communities. *Hispanic Journal of Behavioral Sciences*, 35(1), 103–120. https://doi:10.1177/0739986312463002

Great Schools Partnership. (2013, September 3). Opportunity gap definition. *The Glossary of Educational Reform*. https://www.edglossary.org/opportunity-gap/

Hergenrather, K. C., Rhodes, S. D., Cowan, C. A., Bardoshi, G., & Pula, S. (2009). Photovoice as community-based participatory research: A qualitative review. *American Journal of Health Behavior*, 33, 686–698.

Hernández-Truyol, B., Harris, A., & Valdes, F. (2006). Beyond the first decade: A forward-looking history of LatCrit theory, community and praxis. *Berkeley La Raza LJ*, 17, 169.

Huber, L. P. (2010). Using Latina/o critical race theory (LatCrit) and racist nativism to explore intersectionality in the educational experiences of undocumented Chicana college students. *Educational Foundations*, 24(1–2), 77–96.

Huitt, W. (2001). Humanism and open education. *Educational psychology interactive*. Valdosta State University. http://chiron.valdosta.edu/whuitt/col/affsys/humed.html.

Liou, D. D., & Rojas, L. (2016). Teaching for empowerment and excellence: The transformative potential of teacher expectations in an urban Latina/o classroom. *The Urban Review*, 48(3), 380–402. https://doi:10.1007/s11256-016-0359-8

Luttrell, W. (2010). A camera Is a big responsibility: A lens for analyzing children's visual voices. *Visual Studies*. 25. https://doi:10.1080/1472586X.2010.523274.

Marín, G., Marín, B. V. (1991). *Research with Hispanic populations*. Sage Morales, A., & Delgado, R. (1996). Critical race theory: The cutting edge. *Contemporary Sociology*, 25(3). https://doi:10.2307/2077485

Noguera P. A. (2004). Social capital and the education of immigrant students: Categories and generalizations. *Sociology of Education*, 77(2), 180–183. https://doi:10.1177/003804070407700206

Parkes, K. A., Dredger, K. S., & Hicks, D. (2013). E-Portfolio as a measure of reflective practice. *International Journal of ePortfolio*, 2(2), 99–115. https://www.theijep.com/pdf/IJEP110.pdf

Parkes, K. A., & Kajder, S. (2010). Eliciting and assessing reflective practice: A case study in web 2.0 technologies. *International Journal of Teaching and Learning in Higher Education*, 22(2), 218–228. https://www.isetl.org/ijtlhe

Reese, L., Balzano, S., Gallimore, R., & Goldenberg, C. (1995). The concept of educación: Latino family values and American schooling. *International Journal of Educational Research*, 23, 57–81. https://doi:10.1016/0883-0355(95)93535-4

Rogers, C., & Freiberg, H. J. (1994). *Freedom to learn* (3rd ed.). Macmillan.

Rotherham, A. J. (2011, May 12). The education crisis no one is talking about. *Time*. https://content.time.com/time/nation/article/0,8599,2070930,00.html

Rumberger, R. W., & Rodríguez, G. M. (2011). *Chicano dropouts*. In R. R. Valencia (Ed.), *Chicano school failure and success: Past, present, and future* (3rd ed., pp. 76–98). Routledge.

Saldaña, J. (2009). *The coding manual for qualitative researchers*. Sage.

Sleeter, C., & Bernal, D. (2004). Critical pedagogy, critical race theory, and antiracist education. In J. A. Banks, & C. M. Banks (Eds.), *The handbook of research on multicultural education* (pp. 240–258). Macmillan.

Solórzano, D. G., & Bernal, D. D. (2001). Examining transformational resistance through a critical race and LatCrit theory framework: Chicana and Chicano students in an urban context. *Urban Education*, 36(3), 308–342. https://doi.org/10.1177/0042085901363002

Solórzano, D. G., & Ornelas, A. (2002). A critical race analysis of advanced placement classes: A case of educational inequality. *Journal of Latinos and Education, 1*(4), 215–229. https://doi:10.1207/s1532771xjle0104_2

Stein, G. L., González, L. M., & Huq, N. (2012). Cultural stressors and the hopelessness model of depressive symptoms in Latino adolescents. *Journal of Youth and Adolescence, 41*(10), 1339–1349. https://doi:10.1007/s10964-012-9765-8

Turcios-Cotto, V. Y., & Milan, S. (2013). Racial/ethnic differences in the educational expectations of adolescents: Does pursuing higher education mean something different to Latino students compared to White and Black students? *Journal of Youth and Adolescence, 42*, 1399–1412. https://doi:10.1007/s10964-012-9845-9

U.S. Census Bureau. (2017). Newsroom: Hispanic heritage. https://www.census.gov/newsroom/facts-for-features/2017/hispanic-heritage.html

Valdés, G. (1996). *Con respeto: Bridging the distances between culturally diverse families and schools: An ethnographic portrait*. Teachers College.

Wang, C., & Burris, M. (1994). Empowerment through Photovoice: Portraits of participation. *Health Education Quarterly, 21*(2), 171–186.

Yin, R. K. (2009). *Case study research: Design and methods* (5th ed.). Sage.

Yosso, T. J. (2005) Whose culture has capital? A critical race theory discussion of community cultural wealth, *Race Ethnicity and Education, 8(1)*, 69–91. https://doi:10.1080/1361332052000341006

Appendix 1

Interview Protocols

Student Interview

1. Tell me a little about yourself and your plans after graduation.
2. When your family arrived in the U.S., what were the challenges you experienced?
3. How did obstacles with language impact your experience?
4. Do you struggle with those same issues now? If not, what helped you resolve them?
5. What do you find to be the biggest obstacles in your pursuit of your plans after graduation?
6. What are the sources of support your family provides as you pursue your post-graduation goals?
7. Do you have family members or older friends that have gone to college that offer you support with your education and achieving your plans after graduation?
8. What kind of support does your school offer to prepare you for after graduation?
9. How do you feel supported by your teachers in your class as you advance?
10. What kinds of programs does your school offer to support you as a Latinx student?
11. In what ways do those supports affect your feeling of preparation for college and career?
12. What do you consider your community of support?
13. What kinds of support do you receive from your community as you prepare for college and career?

14. What are you still lacking despite these collective supports?
15. Do you feel prepared for college and career?

Parental Figure Interview

1. Tell me a little about yourself and the plans for your family.
2. When your family arrived in the U.S., what were the challenges you experienced?
3. How did obstacles with language impact your experience?
4. Do you struggle with those same issues now? If not, what helped you resolve them?
5. What do you find to be the biggest obstacles in your pursuit of your plans for your family?
6. What are the sources of support your family provides for your students as they pursue their post-graduation goals?
7. Do you have family members or family friends that have gone to college that offer your child support with their education and achieving their plans after graduation?
8. What kinds of support does your child's school offer to prepare them or you for life after your child graduates?
9. How do you feel your child is supported by his/her teachers?
10. What kinds of programs does your school offer to support you as a Latinx parent?
11. In what ways do those supports affect your feeling of preparation for your child to go to college and career?
12. What do you consider your community of support?
13. What kinds of support do you receive from your community as you prepare your child for college and career?
14. What do you feel is still necessary to ensure your child is prepared for college and career?

Chapter Five

PhotoVoice:
Centering Community-Based Literacies in First-Year Writing

Jennifer Fike and Madina Djuraeva

With strong ties to sociocultural dialogic learning (Freire, 1972), PhotoVoice is a participatory evaluation method with interdisciplinary application. Its goals are to enable people to record and reflect on their community's strengths and concerns, to promote critical dialogue and knowledge about important community issues through large and small group discussions of photographs, and to reach policymakers (Wang & Burris, 1994). Across the disciplines, scholars have highlighted its efficacy in nurturing a sense of belonging, fostering active engagement, and enabling agency specifically among minoritized and marginalized groups. For example, in psychology and health sciences, PhotoVoice supports the observation and development of empowerment and engagement through community agency among oppressed populations and marginalized youth (Delgado, 2015; Foster-Fishman et al., 2005; Strack et al., 2004). In education, PhotoVoice has been given much attention as a research method (see, for example, Latz, 2017; Sutton-Brown, 2014), with a few studies reporting its utility as an instructional method, to fuel student persistence in the field of engineering (Herrera et al., 2023), reflect on writing before and after grading (Esambe et al., 2016), and provide authentic meaningful learning engagements for K-12 teachers and students (Adams & Brooks, 2014; Farley et al., 2017), as well as graduate students (Schell et al., 2009). Building on the existing scholarship on PhotoVoice and its affordances for both research and teaching, this chapter discusses using PhotoVoice as an equity-facilitating instructional method in a first-year writing (FYW) class in a large, metropolitan community college in the central United States.

Using PhotoVoice to Bridge Community Literacies and Academic Writing

It is not unusual to find PhotoVoice used as a complementary writing tool, since students using PhotoVoice are often asked to write an accompanying narrative for their photographs. Findings agree that PhotoVoice assignments can encourage students who are reluctant to write, increase meta-awareness and critical thinking, and foster open discussion regarding students' experiences with instructional methods and their own writing competencies (de lo Ríos, 2020; Esambe et al., 2016; Zenkov & Harmon, 2009). What we contribute to this line of scholarship as a result of our curriculum intervention study is that using PhotoVoice in an FYW class as a lead-in to the first essay helped students bring their out-of-school language and literacy practices into the high-stakes and often exclusionary academic writing context (Inoue, 2015; Matsuda, 2010; Trimbur, 2006). The space and opportunity for students to articulate communal belonging, language, and literacy competencies in first-year college writing promoted greater student engagement and confidence as "new" academic writers.

Participants and Context

The study participants were highly diverse, often multilingual, members of the same 8-week course section of English 1113 within the context of a large, urban community college in the south-central United States. Community colleges aim to increase accessibility and enroll nearly 50% of U.S. undergraduates; however, community college students face significant challenges, especially in required FYW courses, with failure rates even higher than the already typical 40% rate for general college freshmen (American Association of Community Colleges, 2024; Hanson, 2021). Many community college students juggle stressors that can impede their educational goals such as academic underpreparedness, full-time employment, parenthood, and being first-in-family to attend college (Bamberger & Smith, 2023; Goldrick-Rab, 2018; Graves, 2023; Huerta et al., 2022). As the first required college composition course, English 1113 is effectively a gatekeeper (Garrett et al., 2017).

In addition to these systemic barriers, higher education in general and "standardized" writing practices in particular alienate students, especially those from minoritized groups, from their home cultures (Bejarano & Valverde, 2012; O'Shea, 2016) and divorce their language practices from their lived experiences (García & Kleyn, 2016; Smitherman, 1995). In response to these scholarly findings, we incorporated a PhotoVoice assignment as the foundation of the research-informed curriculum intervention instead of beginning with the usual personal narrative essay prompt. As a student-centered, interactive, dialogic experience, PhotoVoice facilitates critical analysis and storytelling, so it was well suited as the first building block of the narrative essay unit. It empowered students to use a culturally relevant (Gay, 2018; Ladson-Billings, 1995) visual medium to explore their discourse communities, allowing for a sense of ownership and access to technology they already possessed on their smartphones.

Data Sources

Data collection was conducted using PhotoVoice as the very first assignment in this 8-week course, introduced through the concept of "discourse communities"—the epistemic and material language used by a specific group (Herzberg, 1986). Following a group discussion in which students were encouraged to share examples of their discourse communities, students took photos of up to three discourse communities to which they belonged, narratively describing their role in them and the language that distinguished each community, and shared them to the class learning management system (LMS) as a sort of virtual gallery. Because the utility and value of discourse communities lie in their connection to students' home cultures, which we aimed to include in their academic writing practices, the PhotoVoice assignment served as a cultural and linguistic bridge between students' out-of-school experiences and their academic writing.

Procedure

As the foundation for the personal narrative essay, PhotoVoice preceded the pre-writing assignments, fostering dialogue throughout the writing process. After discussion with their peers and some guidance from the instructor, students chose one of their discourse communities to write about. From there, students took their chosen picture and were paired with a classmate to conduct semi-structured interviews during which the students explored and explained their discourse community, what kinds of activities they pursued within that community, what types of language were used, and how they saw themselves as a member of that community. Next, students were given a basic outline for a personal narrative essay and drew upon their PhotoVoice activity and interview to develop a story. The essay writing prompt was kept simple and purposefully broad to signal that students had nearly complete agency over their essays. The writing prompt was, "Tell a story about something you learned about yourself as a member of your chosen discourse community." Throughout the writing process, students were regularly given time in class to work alongside their peers and instructor, keeping the class environment student centered.

Researcher Backgrounds

The curriculum intervention and the instructor's involvement played equally important roles in transforming the course. Jennifer, who had over a decade of experience teaching writing in the academic context, was passionate about meeting the needs of her multilingual and multicultural students, whereas Madina, a multilingual educator and researcher, led the research process by guiding its design, co-developing the PhotoVoice assignment, and collecting data to avoid conflict of interest. Together, we combined decades of teaching experiences to demystify and deprivilege "academic" English, positioning it as just one more discourse community to which students belonged.

Discourse Competencies Through the PhotoVoice Lens

Data Analysis

The examples provided below of three students' PhotoVoice assignments and their own words describing their photographs are part of a larger study in which we employed a qualitative, socially situated approach to discourse analysis (Gee, 2007; Vygotsky, 1981). The study examined how students felt about their writing identity and confidence, following assignments that validated out-of-school language practices and displaced exclusive language ideologies common in academic writing contexts. The presented student work below exemplifies how this method validated students' existing language backgrounds and experiences and encouraged them to present themselves as knowledgeable authorities on the subjects they would be writing about in their upcoming essays. We contend that the act of sharing their unique voices and identities established a common ground among the students. Instead of their diversity acting as a separating factor, the PhotoVoice assignment enabled the students to claim their identities as writers while fostering connections across differences. Importantly, the PhotoVoice assignment gave students a platform to reflect upon the activities and language use practices that signaled their belonging to their diverse discourse communities as a parallel to the college writing class.

PhotoVoice 1 *"I feel that I can be my genuine self around them."*

> The discourse community is my family, specifically my uncle and his kids, my cousins. We all share an interest in TV shows and music. I feel that I can be my genuine self around them. I am the far away niece/cousin that still visit and calls when they can. We talk to each other comfortably in English and we have inside jokes that are a little dark but hilarious to us.

> With my uncle and my cousins, we share a dog. I couldn't keep my dog due to moving to a new apartment, to moving states, and to moving states again. I stay in contact to take care of my dog with them watching him. As well as our interest in the TV show Breaking Bad and the anime JoJo's Biazarre Adventure, we are the oddballs of the family. We are also the glue of the family to make sure everyone stays to contact. This discourse language is Spanglish, mostly English for my cousins don't speak Spanish fluently. But I speak to my uncle's mom that only speaks in Spanish. My role is being the far-off cousin and the one with the most memories shared between like the tree. I stay in contact through visits and phone calls.

This student's PhotoVoice submission featured her family, describing the discourse community as one in which she had a highly valued role and multiple language competencies. By sharing her family's multilingual practices—blending English, Spanish, and Spanglish—she reflected on her role in the family being "like the tree" as she stays "in contact through visits and phone calls." In her reflection, we see her as a language broker, providing informal translations to facilitate understanding between family members who speak multiple languages. This ensures equitable engagement and belonging for all members of her family. Her meta-commentary is indexical of her high self-assurance as the most fluent English speaker in her family, as well as her linguistic mastery in Spanish and Spanglish. The PhotoVoice process enabled the transference of her linguistic identity and culture into the college writing context. Just as her family adopted varied language styles to support clear communication in a diverse group, this example serves as an analogy of how a class of students with diverse life experiences and language backgrounds can collectively negotiate language and writing norms for themselves as a newly forming discourse community.

PhotoVoice 2 *"There is a type of way you interact with people."*

> This is a game of Warhammer with all the models set up. Me and my friends mainly talk about the lore and the datasheets of units.
>
> To expand on the thought of Warhammer. It is a game of plastic toy soldiers that you have to build and paint the models then you put them on the table against other. There is a type of way you interact with people with terms like "Deep Strike" which Raven Guard are good at or "Feel No Pain" in which the Dark Elves have that kind of ability to ignored damage.
>
> I learn of the truly the differences of the ways I interact with the groups I'm part of.

This student's PhotoVoice submission focused on his Warhammer miniature wargame setup, highlighting his belonging to a highly specialized gaming discourse community. Through his narrative, he demonstrated metacognitive awareness of the specialized language practices that signal exclusivity and membership. Defining jargon like "Deep Strike" and "Dark Elves," he showed his competency with his community's linguistic norms. His understanding that "there is a type of way you interact" by using specific terminology demonstrates how language use facilitates community belonging and engagement. While some may be quick to judge the content of his narrative as nonacademic, his ability to define terms, provide examples, and analyze his discourse community model core academic writing skills. The PhotoVoice project enabled him to leverage his existing expertise as he acquired new strategies for succeeding in college writing contexts. What is especially significant in his narrative is his developing awareness and ownership of the distinctive language and literacy practices he already possesses. As an equity-minded approach, PhotoVoice empowered this student to demonstrate authoritative language use while developing skills in the emerging discourse community that is his college writing class.

PhotoVoice 3 *"I've been a part of this community since I was about 14 years old."*

> Represented by the picture is the car community. I've been a part of this community since I was about 14 years old, when my father purchased me in 1978 firebird. I've been going to car meets ever since. Most of the meats I go to and talk to people there most people are redneck and have a decent southern drawl. There aren't really roles in the car community unless you are a racer. however, it's usually just guys they like to go hang out with there buddies and talk about cars.

This is another student's PhotoVoice submission of a classic car photograph representing his involvement with a local "car meet" discourse community. He demonstrated critical literacy by analyzing how language can facilitate belonging. Though describing the group's "redneck" and "southern drawl" style of speech could carry negative connotations, the student positioned these as culturally relevant ways of communicating belonging: he was accepted as a young teen and still feels a sense of camaraderie with his "buddies" who "talk about cars" in these ways. In the class, the student's speech did not reflect those markers, indicating that he was able to adapt his language across communities. The student exhibited his competency about cars and his ownership of automotive jargon, self-validating an out-of-school discourse with academic skills like analysis and exemplification. As an equity-facilitating pedagogy, PhotoVoice fostered this student's growth as a writer by affirming his ways of knowing and communicating his values.

PhotoVoice 4 *"We speak in English very casual."*

> This discourse community is one of my workplaces. I work the night shift where it is just two or three of us working at a time. It interchanges between 10 of us, but I work mostly with 6 of my coworkers. We work together well like a well oil machine, we know which task are ours to do to not waste time. We talk about our lives and issues and give advice on what to do with them issues. I work in the smoothie part and we all due drive-through. We speak in English very casual.

This student's PhotoVoice picture is of her workplace. Whereas the topics of discussion are not unique—"our lives and issues," and giving advice—the student implies that she and her coworkers communicate well about their tasks at work so that they can be efficient, speaking "English very casual." This reflection reinforces the arguments referenced earlier in this chapter by demonstrating the power of communal belonging, that is the space and ease of communicating about personal lives and issues while also navigating the professional environment. The student's narrative reveals her understanding of the connection between place and discourse, as it can dictate the purpose of communication. This PhotoVoice facilitated the student's engagement with her role in a workplace discourse community, as bringing others into conversation to accomplish a common goal, and noticing how tone can serve for meaning making. This activity honored the student's place of employment as a valid subject for academic writing while also offering an opportunity to build upon her writing skills.

Affordances and Implications of PhotoVoice in Teaching First-Year Writing

Discussion

The purpose of this chapter was to present the role and utility of PhotoVoice in a first-year writing class in a community college and discuss its affordances as an equity-minded pedagogy, useful in promoting belonging and writing identity formation through student-centered learning, especially as it concerns validation of diverse language practices to de-privilege academic discourse. As we have discussed earlier in this chapter, a number of challenges that arise in the community college writing context stem from the intersection of open admissions policies, language diversities, and a monoglossic language ideology. PhotoVoice afforded an instructional opportunity to disrupt the highly exclusive monolingual environment of a first-year writing class in a community college by centering students' community-based literacies.

The students' PhotoVoice assignments demonstrated that they were part of a number of discourse communities in which they positioned themselves and were positioned by others as competent members and experts of the particular language and literacy practices of those communities: "bilingual extended family," "car meet," "specialized gaming community," and "workplace." The assignment enabled them to reflect on these competencies and revealed confident student voices in writing, such as being "the one with the most memories shared like a tree," awareness of "the differences I interact with the groups I am part of," belonging to the community "since 14 years old," and working well with colleagues by "speaking English very casual." Collectively, the student examples highlight how PhotoVoice tapped into students' natural ability to critically analyze their language practices and evidence of their expertise and community membership and share those roles with their classmates. With guidance from their instructor, students examined the ways in which they integrated into and developed mastery in their discourse communities and could then envision the writing class itself as an emerging discourse community where language norms could be negotiated by students themselves as its members. Additionally, the students demonstrated skills in defining terms, providing examples, and analyzing language use, connecting those skills to their developing academic writing proficiencies as they wrote the narrative descriptions of their photos. PhotoVoice was especially supportive of this identity work, simultaneously supporting students' lived experiences as they affirmed their new belonging as college writers. Honoring and building upon the diversity, that is students' diverse language and literacy practices, as a legitimate academic writing asset is what made PhotoVoice an equity-facilitating instructional tool in this study.

Implications

The combination of using PhotoVoice as both an instructional and research method provided a window into the meaningful communities and practices that can influence students' identities as new college writers. Approaching PhotoVoice with a research mindset required thorough planning to effectively utilize it in a way that facilitated analysis, suggesting PhotoVoice has excellent utility at the outset of pedagogical research projects to heighten student engagement as they discover personal connections to discipline-specific topics. The creative and student-centered instructional use of PhotoVoice has implications for the development of more inclusive writing pedagogies that could capitalize on students' self-awareness of their discourse community memberships as an asset and recognize linguistic creativity and negotiation as key academic skills. Future qualitative research could explore how utilizing culturally relevant practices might support students' transitions into new academic contexts, including postsecondary writing genres. Additionally, quantitative studies could examine whether this type of asset-based pedagogical approach could impact long-term educational outcomes like persistence.

Conclusion

To conclude, the analysis of students' PhotoVoice reveals a need to consider broader definitions of cultural relevance to validate diversity and expertise in the class. While scholars and educators of equity-focused pedagogies often emphasize ethnicity, race, and named languages, these PhotoVoice examples show that cultural diversity also stems from students' activities, hobbies, employment, and family practices, all of which shape identities, ways of knowing, and community-specific language use. In the community college setting, attending to students' various language and literacy experiences supports efforts in developing equitable learning, which is especially important given the diversity across age, race, ethnicity, language, and college preparedness. PhotoVoice could facilitate student transitions into academic subject-specific discourse communities by helping students develop meaningful connections between their existing and developing communities. Overall, this study calls for such learning experiences as vital to facilitate student success and fulfill the democratic mission of open-access higher education.

References

Adams, S., & Brooks, K. (2014). Using Photovoice to empower K-12 teachers and students through authentic literacy engagements. *Writing and Pedagogy, 6*(3), 649–664. doi: http://www.equinoxpub.com/journals/index.php/WAP/article/view/18582

American Association of Community Colleges. (2024, May 1). *Fast Facts*. https://www.aacc.nche.edu/research-trends/fast-facts/?_gl=1*mdvnqo*_ga*NTQxOTg1NDA3LjE2ODEyNjc5MjI.*_up*MQ.

Bamberger, M. R., & Smith, T. J. (2023). First-generation college students: Goals and challenges of community college. *Community College Review, 51*(3), 445–462. https://doi.org/10.1177/00915521231163903

Bejarano, C., & Valverde, M. (2012). From the fields to the university: Charting educational access and success for farmworker students using a community cultural wealth framework. *Association of Mexican American Educators Journal, 6*(2).

Delgado, M. (2015). *Urban youth and Photovoice: Visual ethnography in action*. Oxford University Press.

de los Ríos, C. V. (2020). Writing oneself into the curriculum: Photovoice journaling in a secondary ethnic studies course. *Written Communication, 37*(4), 487–511. https://doi.org/10.1177/0741088320938794

Esambe, E., Mosito, C., & Pather, S. (2016). First-year students' essay writing practices: Formative feedback and interim literacies. *Reading and Writing*, 7(1), 1–11.

Farley, L. A., Brooks, K., & Pope, K. (2017). Engaging students in praxis using Photovoice research. *Multicultural Education*, 24(2), 49–52.

Foster-Fishman, P., Nowell, B., Deacon, Z., Nievar, M. A., and McCann, P. (2005). Using methods that matter: The impact of reflection, dialogue, and voice. *American Journal of Community Psychology*, 36(3–4), 275–291. https://doi.org/10.1007/s10464-005-8626-y

Freire, P. (1972). *Pedagogy of the oppressed*. Continuum.

García, O., & Kleyn, T. (2016). *Translanguaging with multilingual students: Learning from classroom moments*. Routledge. https://www.routledge.com/Translanguaging-with-Multilingual-Students-Learning-from-Classroom-Moments/Garcia-Kleyn/p/book/9781138906983

Garrett, N., Bridgewater, M., & Feinstein, B. (2017). How student performance in first-year composition predicts retention and overall student access. In T. Ruecker, D. Shepherd, H. Estrem, and B. Brunk-Chavez (Eds.), *Retention, persistence, and writing programs* (pp. 93–113). Utah State University Press.

Gay, G. (2018). *Culturally responsive teaching: Theory, research, and practice*. Teachers College Press. https://upcolorado.com/utah-state-university-press/item/3116-retention-persistence-and-writing-programs

Gee, J. (2007). *Social linguistics and literacies: Ideology in discourses*. Routledge. https://doi.org/10.4324/9780203944806

Goldrick-Rab, S. (2018). Addressing community college completion rates by securing students' basic needs: New directions for community colleges. *New Directions for Community Colleges, (184)*, 7–16. https://doi.org/10.1002/cc.20323

Graves, D. L. (2023). Latinx community college students experiencing financial aid income verification: A critical race analysis. *EdWorkingPaper, 22-599*. Annenberg Institute at Brown University:

Hanson, M. (2021). *College dropout rates*. Education data initiative. https://educationdata.org/college-dropout-rates

Herrera, L., Schaefer, K. L., Benjamin, L. S. S., & Henderson, J. A. (2023). Flash on: Capturing minoritized engineering students' persistence through Photovoice research. *Sustainability*, 15(6), Article 6. https://doi.org/10.3390/su15065311

Herzberg, B. (1986). The politics of discourse communities. *Conference on College Composition and Communication,* New Orleans, LA.

Huerta, A. H., Ríos-Aguilar, C., & Ramírez, D. (2022). "I had to figure it out": A case study of how community college student parents of color navigate college and careers. *Community College Review*, 50(2), 193–218. https://doi.org/10.1177/00915521211061425

Inoue, A. B. (2015). *Antiracist writing assessment ecologies: Teaching and assessing writing for a socially just future*. The WAC Clearinghouse; Parlor Press. https://doi.org/10.37514/PER-B.2015.0698

Ladson-Billings, G. (1995). Toward a theory of culturally relevant pedagogy. *American*

Educational Research Journal, 32(3), 465–491.

Latz, A. O. (2017). *Photovoice research in education and beyond: A practical guide from theory to exhibition*. Routledge. https://doi.org/10.4324/9781315724089

Matsuda, P. K. (2010). The myth of linguistic homogeneity in U.S. college composition. In B. Horner, M.-Z. Lu, and P. K. Matsuda (Eds.), *Cross-language relations in composition* (pp. 81–96). Southern Illinois University Press.

O'Shea, S. (2016). Avoiding the manufacture of 'sameness': First-in-family students, cultural capital and the higher education environment. *High Education (72)*, 59–78. https://doi.org/10.1007/s10734-015-9938-y

Schell, K., Ferguson, A., Hamoline, R., Shea, J., & Thomas-MacLean, R. (2009). Photovoice as a teaching tool: Learning by doing with visual methods. *International Journal of Teaching and Learning in Higher Education, 21*(3), 340–352.

Smitherman, G. (1995). Students' right to their own language: A retrospective. *The English Journal, 84*(1), 21–27. https://doi.org/10.2307/820470

Strack, R. W., Magill, C., & McDonagh, K. (2004). Engaging youth through Photovoice. *Health Promotion Practice, 5*(1), 49–58.

Sutton-Brown, C. A. (2014). Photovoice: A methodological guide. *Photography and Culture, 7*(2), 169–185. https://doi.org/10.2752/175145214X13999922103165

Trimbur, J. (2006). Linguistic memory and the politics of the U.S. English. *College English, 68*(6), 575–588. https://doi.org/10.2307/25472176

Vygotsky, L. S. (1981). *Mind in society: The development of higher psychological processes*. Harvard University Press.

Wang, C., & Burris, M. A. (1994). Empowerment through photo novella: Portraits of participation. *Health Education Quarterly, 21*(2), 171–186. https://doi.org/10.1177/109019819402100204

Zenkov, K., & Harmon, J. (2009). Picturing a writing process: Photovoice and teaching writing to urban youth. *Journal of Adolescent & Adult Literacy, 52*(7), 575–584. https://doi.org/10.1598/JAAL.52.7.3

CHAPTER SIX

Visual Voices:

Students' Journey From Exploration to Activism Through PhotoVoice in the Borderlands

Elizabeth Astorga Gaxiola

Introduction/Background

For some time now, I've been employing arts-based teaching methods in my undergraduate classes, initially at the University of Arizona and presently at Pima Community College. These courses incorporate a social justice aspect, and utilizing arts-based approaches (Burgard et al., 2021) has been essential. This allows students to express themselves through art rather than traditional written assignments. Incorporating these arts-based methods can transform the learning experience for students by providing them with alternative mediums for learning, self-reflection, and engagement. These teaching methods also promote creativity and innovation, skills that are necessary in today's technological world, as well as being socially mindful members of their communities.

I was first introduced to a PhotoVoice study that was written by scholars of the University of North Carolina. They employed this research method to examine and address the impact of immigration (I started to explore additional studies utilizing PhotoVoice, and what caught my attention the most was the effectiveness of this approach when employing photography as its medium. PhotoVoice not only facilitates the exploration of community dynamics but empowers researchers to uncover, depict, and deepen an understanding of a community (Wang, 1999).

Consequently, I began incorporating this research methodology into my teaching practices at Pima Community College with the aim of cultivating critical thinking and fostering creative expression among my students (Lorenz & Bush, 2022). This approach was integrated into the curriculum of a Mexican American Culture and History course, providing students with a unique opportunity to explore the issues that impact our Latinx communities through a hands-on participatory research process. By integrating this methodology into the curriculum, I sought to empower students to not only deepen their understanding of the social injustices that impact our communities, but also to develop essential skills in teamwork, communication, critical and analytical skills, and creative expression, ultimately fostering a learning experience that is more dynamic and rewarding.

Located amidst the stunning scenery of the Southwestern United States, Pima Community College serves the Tucson, Arizona area and its surroundings, providing educational opportunities to a student body of approximately 17,000 individuals in fall 2022. The college's demographic makeup comprises 48.2% Hispanic or Latino, 36.5% white, 4.61% Black or African American, 2.84% Asian, 2.77% two or More Races, 1.88% American Indian or Alaska Native, and 0.34% Native Hawaiian or Other Pacific Islanders. The course where PhotoVoice is applied is predominantly attended by Latinx students. According to a report by Billot et al. (2023), Tucson's population as of the 2020 census is 42.2% Hispanic or Latino. In the forthcoming paragraphs, I outline the different steps presented to students for starting and completing their projects.

Introducing Students to the PhotoVoice Framework

On the first day of the semester, I acquaint students with the midterm PhotoVoice group project that they will undertake. I demonstrate different forms and methods of activism and introduce them to topics that historically have impacted Latinx communities on a global scale. It is important to introduce students to this because it contextualizes the relevance and significance of the PhotoVoice project within broader social dynamics. Additionally, introducing topics that impact communities provides students with insight into real-world issues and challenges, illustrating the potential impact their PhotoVoice project can have in addressing or raising awareness about these issues.

In the following class session, students are grouped together to work collaboratively on the PhotoVoice project alongside their peers. These groups are selected randomly to ensure varied teams. I then begin by introducing students to the concept of PhotoVoice through a presentation that serves as a thorough overview, covering various aspects of PhotoVoice. Initially, we examine the definition of PhotoVoice, which is characterized as a collaborative effort where individuals come together, utilizing photography as a medium to construct a collective narrative surrounding a community issue or challenge (Liebenberg, 2018). We then explore the purpose behind PhotoVoice, which is highlighted as a stimulus for critical dialogue (Ogunnusi, 2019), tapping into the power of visuals to activate conversations (Andina-Diaz, 2020; Downey et al., 2009) and drive positive change within communities (Liebenberg, 2022). This visual research methodology isn't just about capturing moments; it's about fostering social transformation (Budig et al., 2018).

Next, we examine the profound impact of PhotoVoice as a tool for empowerment, especially for those whose voices often go unheard (Foster-Fishman et al., 2005). By equipping individuals with cameras and inviting them to share their stories through pictures and words, PhotoVoice highlights the perspectives of underrepresented communities, empowering them to advocate for their needs (Walls & Holquist, 2019). This heightens students' awareness of their environment. It enables them to step into the role of researchers, gathering and analyzing data to address challenges effectively. Through this process, students gain the tools and opportunities needed to empower their own voices (Goodhart et al., 2006).

I continue to inform students how PhotoVoice was developed and share that in the 1990s, the concept of PhotoVoice took shape through the collaborative efforts of Professor Caroline Wang, based at the University of Michigan School of Public Health, and Mary Ann Burris, affiliated with the Ford Foundation. Their aim was to bridge the gap between the lived experiences of rural women in Yunnan Province, China and the decision-making processes concerning regional development (Wang et al., 1998). Drawing inspiration from various sources, Wang and Burris crafted PhotoVoice as a methodological approach. Their design incorporated elements from Paulo Freire's concept of "critical consciousness," which encourages individuals to critically examine and challenge their social realities (Freire, 1970). Additionally, they integrated insights from feminist theory, which emphasizes the importance of amplifying underrepresented voices, particularly those of women. Combining these influences, Wang and Burris developed PhotoVoice in 1992, positioning it as a tool to empower communities by allowing them to visually articulate their perspectives and advocate for change through the medium of photography.

In summary, PhotoVoice emerges as more than just a photographic technique; it represents a narrative of empowerment, enlightenment, and advocacy, bringing together the diverse voices and visions of communities in working towards different and better circumstances. In Figure 6.1, you will find the PhotoVoice process that we use in our courses.

Figure 6.1 *Process used for PhotoVoice*

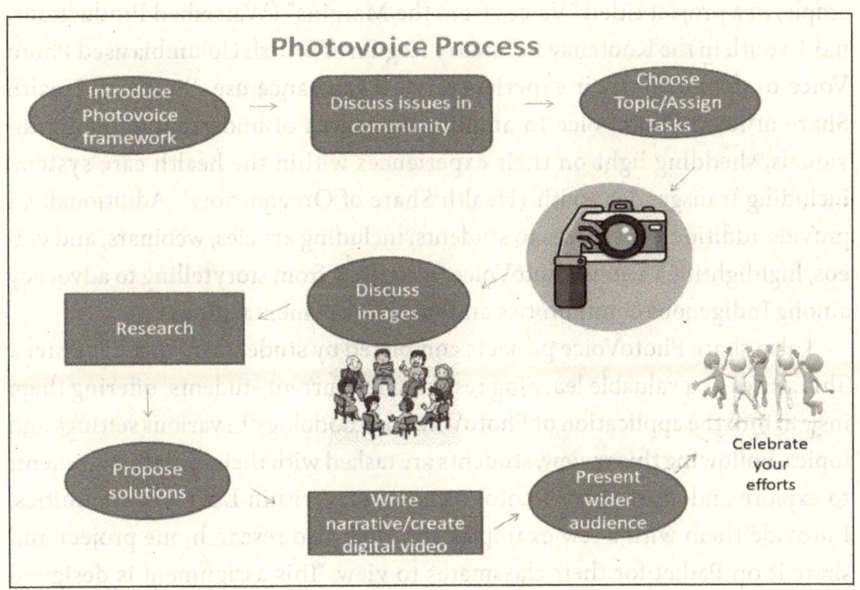

Prior Projects

During class, I introduce students to various PhotoVoice projects created by community members globally and discuss the impact and significance of them. For example, one project involved youth promoting better hygiene practices within their families and communities through PhotoVoice. The "Stop Diarrhea Initiative" (Reckitt, 2018) empowered children to prompt change within their localities, aiming to eliminate diarrhea as a leading cause of death by 2020. An illustrative video by a young participant named Manisha provides a moving narrative through images, detailing her life in Kolkata, India and the transformative effect of the PhotoVoice initiative on her community. A second initiative led by Associate Professor Leanne Charlesworth in 2011 was a PhotoVoice exhibition that shed light on homelessness in Rochester, New York. This exhibition, titled "Exposed: Rochester's Hidden Victims of Homelessness," offered a platform for members of the homeless community to convey their daily struggles and living conditions.

Further examples feature the diverse applications of PhotoVoice. For example, in a project titled "Voices from the Margins" (Watershed Productions, n.d.), youth in the Kootenay Boundary Region of British Columbia used Photo Voice to document their experiences with substance use. Similarly, Health Share utilized PhotoVoice to amplify the voices of underrepresented individuals, shedding light on their experiences within the health care system, including transgender youth (Health Share of Oregon, 2017). Additionally, I provide additional resources to students, including articles, webinars, and videos, highlighting various PhotoVoice initiatives, from storytelling to advocacy among Indigenous communities and survivors of mental illness.

I also share PhotoVoice projects completed by students in prior semesters. This serves as a valuable learning resource for current students, offering them insight into the application of PhotoVoice methodology in various settings and topics. Following this review, students are tasked with their initial assignment: to explore and share other PhotoVoice projects within Latinx communities. I provide them with a few examples and they also research one project and share it on Padlet for their classmates to view. This assignment is designed to deepen their understanding of the research method within these specific cultural contexts.

Dialogue

After introducing the PhotoVoice methodology as a form of participatory action research and showcasing videos on activism, the students and I collectively initiate a dialogue focusing on the pressing concerns within their communities. I prompt them with questions aimed at identifying issues that hold personal significance: What community challenges affect you, your family, friends, and neighbors, or have influenced your ancestors? What issue weighs heavily on your mind, keeping you awake at night? Moreover, I encourage them to see themselves as catalysts for change, as scholars and activists, considering the challenges affecting Latinx communities that they aim to raise awareness of and propose solutions for.

Tasks

Students are advised that their project will be a collaborative effort undertaken in groups, typically consisting of three to four students. Through the lens of photography, they document the conditions related to their chosen issue and brainstorm potential solutions. Subsequently, they learn that their findings will be presented in a digital format. Initially, students are hesitant about creating a digital video, but I ask them, how many TikTokers are in the house? Nearly everyone raises their hand in response. I then reassure them that they are experts in digital editing, easing the stress associated with the assignment. Furthermore, students are offered the opportunity to participate in a workshop conducted by a skilled staff member proficient in creating digital videos. This option aims to provide additional support and guidance to students who may require assistance in navigating the digital video creating process. They compile a video using the collected photographs and present it to the class, detailing their chosen topic, showcasing the photographs, discussing their research findings, and suggesting solutions to the issues they studied. They might also select images as metaphors in their digital videos. For instance, in Image 1, a student used it to express their struggle with "identity crisis," feeling neither fully Mexican nor American enough. Another instance of exploring identity is evident in Image 2, where a student addresses similar concerns.

Image 1 *Identity crisis*

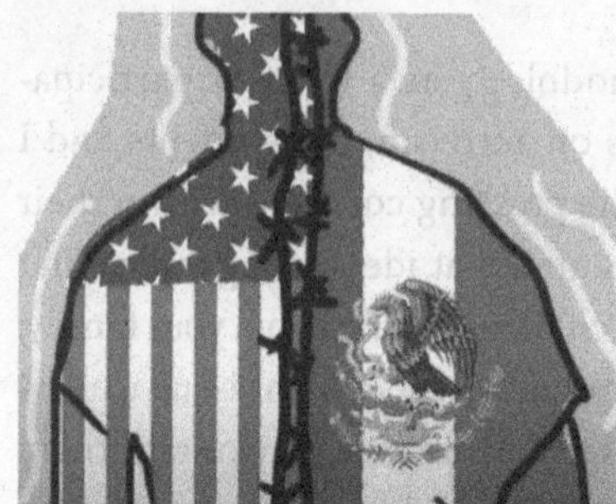

Image 2 *Identity exploration*

Students are advised to begin by exchanging contact details and establishing a shared document to facilitate idea sharing. They are tasked with collectively selecting a topic of interest and dividing responsibilities among group members. For instance, one student may focus on narration, another on creating the digital video, while everyone contributes to capturing photos and conducting research.

During class sessions, students are allotted limited time to gather and prepare for the assignment. Due to time constraints, students meet outside of class, gathering in cafes or restaurants, or virtually, to collaborate further on their project. To foster collaboration and build rapport, their teams are consistently grouped together for various class activities at the beginning of the semester, enabling them to become acquainted with one another.

The Research

While some students opt to work independently photographing their community, others like to explore with their group. Many have expressed their preference to explore alongside friends or family members. Before they go out to the community, I emphasize the importance of ethical principles in research. I share guidelines emphasizing respect, transparency, cultural sensitivity, integrity, humility, and a commitment to personal and professional responsibilities (Jamshidi et al., 2014). These principles serve as a foundation for conducting ethical and responsible research within the community.

In the forthcoming paragraphs, I outline the various topics students have chosen for their PhotoVoice projects. Over the past five semesters, students have created 50 PhotoVoice projects covering a wide range of topics. As previously noted, these topics were selected by the students based on the issues that are important or impact them, their families, friends, or members of their communities. From the 50 projects, the three main topics that students conveyed impacted them or their Latinx communities were: (1) educational disparities; (2) the impact of homelessness; and (3) mental health challenges. Additionally, other topics were issues such as machismo, gender roles, immigration policies, gun violence, and substance abuse. Other topics included language barriers, gentrification, cultural appropriation, infrastructure disparities, inflation, stereotypes, and the economic effects of COVID-19 along the United States–Mexico border.

Education

The focus on unequal access to quality education and academic opportunities among Latinx students was one of the main topics students conveyed were important to them. Latinx students often encounter barriers that limit their access to resources, funding, and equitable educational outcomes compared to their peers from non-Latinx backgrounds (Acevedo-Gil, 2019). One aspect that students explored was the disparities in resources and funding between Latinx-majority schools and schools serving predominantly non-Latinx populations in the communities they reside in. They highlighted how Latinx-majority schools have fewer resources, including limited access to technology, deteriorating infrastructure (see Image 3), and insufficient funding for extracurricular activities. They noted that these disparities perpetuate inequities in educational opportunities.

Image 3 *School infrastructure*

Additionally, students also documented the impact of language barriers, cultural differences, and discrimination on the educational experiences of Latinx youth. Language barriers can impede academic success by limiting access to English-language instruction and support services for English language learners, especially for the migrant population (Rana, 2024). Cultural differences may not always be recognized or valued in educational settings, leading to alienation among Latinx students (Irizarry, 2017). Moreover, discrimination and bias, whether explicit or subtle, can negatively affect Latinx students' academic performance, self-esteem, and sense of belonging in school environments (Brown & Tam, 2019).

They also highlighted the resilience and academic aptitude of Latinx students despite facing systemic barriers, such as lack of financial resources, systemic discrimination, lack of support by teachers (Manzano-Sanchez et al., 2019), and immigration and language issues (Valenzuela et al., 2012). Through their photography and digital videos, students emphasized these disparities and raised awareness to the educational inequities they found in their research, witnessed, or experienced. Many of these projects were very personal, such as one student who explored the intersection of poverty and education and the difficulties faced by her family (see Image 4). In this project, students provided statistical information on poverty rates and how it impacts students, such as having to drop out of high school to work and help their families financially. They also provided information on the lack of funding in their schools to sustain cultural programs, such as music and dance.

Image 4 *Poverty and education PhotoVoice project*

Through their PhotoVoice projects, students made suggestions for policy changes and community initiatives aimed at addressing these systemic inequalities in education in order for all students, regardless of background, to have access to quality education and opportunities for academic success. These projects have been presented in different venues, such as conferences and symposiums where faculty, college administrators, staff, community members and local politicians have been in attendance.

Homelessness

The impact of homelessness in Latinx communities was the second highest concern for students. In their PhotoVoice projects, they explored the multifaceted challenges faced by individuals and families experiencing homelessness in Latinx communities and societal failure to address basic human protections and secure human needs (Moya et al., 2017). One aspect they discovered is the difficulty in finding stable housing. They found that individuals experiencing homelessness often encounter obstacles in securing safe and affordable housing options, due to factors such as discrimination, limited access to rental assistance programs, insufficient income to afford housing due to inflation, and the trickle effect of the COVID pandemic (Albon et al., 2020; Rodriguez et al., 2022).

Through the use of photography, research, videos, and interviews, students explored the root causes of homelessness among Latinx populations (Ji, 2006; Knight, 2024). They depicted scenes illustrating the struggles of finding shelter, accessing services, and navigating their local community while experiencing homelessness (see Images 5 and 6).

Image 5 *Homelessness PhotoVoice project*

Overall, exploring the impact of homelessness in Latinx communities through photography and their digital videos provided visual narratives that humanize the issue and underscore the urgent need for systemic solutions to address housing insecurity and support for the homeless in our communities. One student mentioned,

> In our PhotoVoice project, homelessness in Tucson became the focal point because it resonated deeply with all of us. Witnessing this issue firsthand or simply caring about its impact on our community fueled our desire to make a difference. Giving a voice to those experiencing homelessness and raising awareness were paramount.

Image 6 *Homeless in the Tucson community*

Mental Health

The topic of mental health was amongst the three highest topics that students mentioned were important to them. They explored the complexities of mental health challenges and the barriers preventing Latinx individuals from accessing appropriate care. Students noted how Latinx communities often face unique obstacles in addressing mental health concerns, stemming from a combination of cultural, socioeconomic, language, and systemic factors (Lee et al., 2022). Several student projects explored the cultural stigma (Choi et al., 2019) surrounding mental illness within these communities, such as how mental health issues are often perceived as taboo topics and how individuals may feel shame or fear of judgment when discussing their struggles. They conveyed how this stigma may raise isolation, reluctance to seek help, and a lack of understanding or support from family members. Students aimed to shed light on the stigma surrounding mental health and challenges by sharing their own personal experiences and interviews with their family members, friends, and group partners.

Moreover, students aimed to promote awareness, reduce stigma, and advocate for culturally competent mental health services, specifically the need for representation of counselors and medical/psychiatric staff tailored to the needs of Latinx individuals and families. They mentioned that by having experienced culturally competent medical staff, they would better understand and respect cultural beliefs, values, and practices of Latinx communities while providing accessible and effective mental health support (Magaña, 2020). By showcasing these experiences and needs in their PhotoVoice projects, students sought to advocate for greater investment in mental health resources and services that are inclusive, linguistically accessible, and culturally sensitive.

Additional topics

Other prominent issues explored through the students' PhotoVoice projects within the Latinx community, included machismo, gender roles, immigration policies, gun violence, and substance abuse. In their research, one group referred to machismo as a cultural concept of masculinity predominant in Latinx communities, often characterized by traits such as dominance, and the expectation of men to fulfill traditional gender roles as providers and protectors (Valdez et al., 2023). These PhotoVoice projects, including one titled "Machismo in the Queer Community," explored the ways in which these norms influence interpersonal dynamics, family structures, and societal expectations within Latinx communities. It is important to raise awareness to help challenge and dismantle harmful stereotypes and promote inclusivity and acceptance within these communities.

Image 7 *Machismo PhotoVoice project*

Several projects also focused on the impact of immigration policies, particularly for individuals and families navigating the complexities of migration and the surveillance in border communities. These projects focused on the lived experiences of immigrants, including the challenges of border enforcement, especially in their experiences in border checkpoints, detention, and family separation due to deportation. They also highlighted the systemic injustices and human rights violations as a result of exclusionary immigration policies. See Image 8 as an example of an exclusionary policy. The wall and concertina wire serve as physical barriers that send a message that certain people or groups are excluded from entering the United States.

Image 8 *Concertina wire on the border wall, Nogales, Arizona*

Through their PhotoVoice projects, students aimed to amplify their own voices and their families' experiences and advocate for support for immigrant and human rights. For example, students worked on a PhotoVoice project to bring awareness to the militarization of their home community in the U.S. and Mexico border region. Image 9 shows a blimp flying over the Nogales border. This is a type of aerial surveillance by the border patrol who were manning the blimp 24 hours per day, 7 days a week. One student explained how she felt with this new aerial surveillance patrolling her community.

> As you walk around Nogales, you can immediately see the white air ship sitting afloat. When driving my vehicle, it seemed as though the blimp was going along with me. It was a strange feeling. It felt

> intrusive. It feels as if you are being observed all the time. The border has become intimidating. (See Images 10 and 11.)

Image 9 *Aerial surveillance at the border*

Image 10 *Surveillance tower*

Image 11 *Border patrol patrolling in Nogales, AZ*

Gun violence was also an important topic for students. One project highlighted the student's experience with gun violence and the efforts made to leave a detrimental lifestyle. A different one highlighted the devastating impact of gun violence in their university community (see Image 12) and the devastating impact on students, families, and their wider community. One student mentioned,

> My group chose the topic of gun violence in Tucson because it was something we all felt passionate about as an issue that desperately needed attention. This is important to me because I grew up going

> to school in a time when school shootings were common and it was normal to be scared of being a victim of gun violence at school. It is heartbreaking and should change.

These projects highlighted the efforts to prevent gun violence through community-based interventions and advocacy for stricter gun control legislation. By raising awareness and promoting dialogue on gun violence prevention, students aimed to contribute to awareness and efforts to create safer communities. An average of 1228 people died and 919 were wounded by guns in Arizona, which is the 31st highest rate of gun violence in the United States (EveryStat, n.d.).

Image 12 *Gun violence at a local university*

Another topic that was important to students was the impact of illegal substances such as fentanyl and substance abuse in their Latinx communities and personal narratives of addiction to vaping. They depicted the complexities of addiction, including underlying causes and consequences, and also the considerable number of vendors offering vaping products. Students showcased how they found and visited a substantial quantity of stores that sold vaping products in their local community. They noted how easy it was for youth to go into these stores to purchase vaping products. See Image 13 of vaping products at a local vendor. Through their PhotoVoice projects, students aimed to raise awareness and advocate for compassionate and comprehensive approaches to addressing the fentanyl crisis and substance abuse, recognizing the urgent need for heightened awareness, especially among youth in their communities.

Image 13 *Vaping products*

Other PhotoVoice topics students chose were language barriers, gentrification, digital gentrification, digital accessibility, disparities of road infrastructure, inflation, cultural appropriation, stereotypes, and the economic effects of COVID-19 along the United States–Mexico border. The PhotoVoice projects on language barriers depicted the ways in which language limitations impact access to education, health care, employment, and social services. They highlighted the importance of language access and interpretation services in promoting equitable access to resources and opportunities within Latinx communities. A student mentioned,

> We focused on the difficulties Spanish speaking families face when receiving medical care and struggles within the education system. It was important to me because this is an issue many families go through daily and goes unnoticed. Since my group has been affected by this obstacle directly and indirectly, it was easily relatable. I wanted to spread awareness of how one can truly be impacted by not receiving the proper care in the medical field or in the classroom and ways we can offer change.

Gentrification was also an important topic for students. Their PhotoVoice projects on gentrification documented the changes (see Image 14) occurring in gentrifying neighborhoods, such as rising housing costs, and especially highlighted the displacement of longtime residents and small businesses in their Latinx communities. Through their projects, they raised awareness about the complexities of gentrification and advocated for policies and strategies that prioritize affordable housing and community preservation. One student mentioned,

> Our group chose to work with gentrification in Latinx communities in Tucson because we think it is an ongoing issue that affects the traditions and quality of life. It was important to me because it helped me understand more about the history of the city and how Latinx communities are being displaced and lack spaces curated for them.

Image 14 *Gentrification in Tucson*

Another topic that was important to students was digital gentrification and digital accessibility. They mentioned how the digital gap was very apparent for low-income versus higher income as well as from elders to youth. They proposed solutions for public and private sectors to invest in promoting digital literacy programs and the need for universal internet access. They felt that digital inclusion and equity would be addressed by broadband internet access in their communities. These are a few images from their PhotoVoice project to showcase the widespread use of technology in their communities; see Images 15 and 16.

Image 15 *Digital gentrification, McDonald's*

Image 16 *Digital gentrification, Walmart*

Another example of the lack of digital accessibility is the use of tablets in medical offices, making it difficult for patients who are not familiar with technology and the requirement to complete medical forms online. A student captured a photograph (see Image 17) of his grandfather, who at 3:30 a.m. was trying to fill out a medical form he had forgotten to complete for an upcoming appointment. The student mentioned how his grandfather was frustrated with the lack of technological knowledge, which caused him stress. The student mentioned, "Health care needs to be accessible. What happens to people who do not have children or grandchildren to help them with technology?"

Image 17 *Lack of digital accessibility*

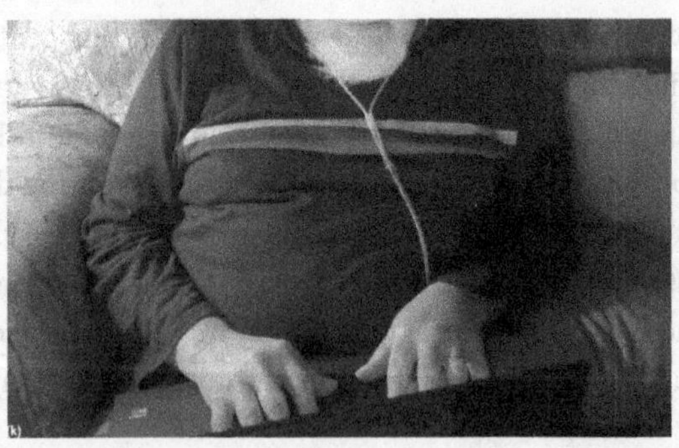

Final Thoughts

The journey through PhotoVoice projects undertaken by students at Pima Community College illuminates the transformative power of visual storytelling as a catalyst for bringing awareness and social change. One student mentioned,

> I have always been attracted to photography and videography, so personally I was excited to have the opportunity to create something educational with this medium. I think it encourages us to get involved more intimately with our community and it engages us with the issues around us. It is easy for us to google a topic and read about it but it becomes more personal once you get out there and get involved.

Embedded within each digital video on their PhotoVoice exploration is a moving account of the social injustices that surround our Latinx communities, such as disparities in our road infrastructure, impact of inflation, environmental concerns, immigration detention centers, stereotyping, discrimination, occupational inequalities, and such. As these students navigated the issues impacting them and their communities, they captured the complexities but also enlightened their advocacy efforts. Their PhotoVoice projects serve as a testament to the power of storytelling, the importance of representation, and the capacity of students to drive meaningful change within their communities. One student mentioned,

> Photography transformed from a camera to a powerful research tool. Through the lens, we captured stories statistics couldn't express, gaining a deeper understanding of the realities of homelessness in Tucson. Looking at the pictures was another impactful takeaway. We saw the shared struggles faced by many experiencing homelessness, but also the diversity of their individual stories.

As these PhotoVoice projects are shared in our class, in our community, and beyond, they serve as a call to action, a call to dismantle barriers, challenge stereotypes, and foster environments of inclusivity and equity. These projects were viewed by many audience members (students, faculty, family, friends, and community members) in conferences and symposiums, who on many occasions mentioned that they were very impacted by the PhotoVoice projects and made them realize that they too could make a difference in their communities by bringing awareness to issues that are important to them.

For these students, conducting their PhotoVoice projects was not just an academic exercise; they were acts of compassion, consciousness raising, and solidarity. One student mentioned,

> Using photography as a research method made me realize how much meaning a picture can hold. When taking pictures, you can feel the emotions and understand what they are going through.

They are a testament to the transformative potential of education and the love they have for their communities. As I reflect on the journey of our students, it reminds me that every image, video, and word they shared and voiced is a catalyst for hope in our Latinx communities. As these remarkable student scholars and activists continue their academic journey, I feel confident that they will "seguir en la lucha" (continue the fight) for an equitable and just future.

References

Acevedo-Gil, N. (2019). College-going facultad: Latinx students anticipating postsecondary institutional obstacles. *Journal of Latinos and Education, 18*(2), 107–125.

Albon, D., Soper, M., & Haro, A. (2020). Potential implications of the COVID-19 pandemic on the homeless population. *Chest, 158*(2), 477–478.

Andina-Díaz, E. (2020). Using Photovoice to stimulate critical thinking: An exploratory study with nursing students. *Revista Latino-Americana de Enfermagem, 28*, e3314.

Brown, C. S., & Tam, M. (2019). Ethnic discrimination predicting academic attitudes for Latinx students in middle childhood. *Journal of Applied Developmental Psychology, 65*, 101061.

Budig, K., Diez, J., Conde, P., Sastre, M., Hernán, M., & Franco, M. (2018). Photovoice and empowerment: Evaluating the transformative potential of a participatory action research project. *BMC Public Health, 18*, 1–9.

Burgard, K. L., O'Quinn, C., Boucher, M. L., Pinnix, N., Trejo, C., & Dickson, C. (2021). Using photographs to create culturally relevant classrooms: People of San Antonio, Texas, in the 1930s. *Social Studies and the Young Learner, 33*(3), 3–7.

Choi, N. Y., Kim, H. Y., & Gruber, E. (2019). Mexican American women college students' willingness to seek counseling: The role of religious cultural values, etiology beliefs, and stigma. *Journal of Counseling Psychology, 66*(5), 577.

Downey, L. H., Ireson, C. L., & Scutchfield, F. D. (2009). The use of Photovoice as a method of facilitating deliberation. *Health Promotion Practice, 10*(3), 419–427. EveryStat. (n.d.). *Gun violence in Arizona.*

EveryStat.org. https://everystat.org/wp-content/uploads/2019/10/Gun-Violence-in-Arizona-2.pdf

Foster-Fishman, P., Nowell, B., Deacon, Z., Nievar, M. A., & McCann, P. (2005). Using methods that matter: The impact of reflection, dialogue, and voice. *American Journal of Community Psychology, 36*, 275–291. Freire, P. (1970). *Pedagogy of the oppressed.* Seabury Press.

Goodhart, F. W., Hsu, J., Baek, J. H., Coleman, A. L., Maresca, F. M., & Miller, M. B. (2006). A view through a different lens: Photovoice as a tool for student advocacy. *Journal of American College Health, 55*(1), 53–56.

Health Share of Oregon. (2017, September 22). *Photovoice* [Video]. YouTube. https://www.youtube.com/watch?v=pXEWGqBnIhs

Irizarry, J. G. (2017). For us, by us. *Culturally sustaining pedagogies: Teaching and learning for justice in a changing world*, 83–98.

Jamshidi, E., Morasae, E. K., Shahandeh, K., Majdzadeh, R., Seydali, E., Aramesh, K., & Abknar, N. L. (2014). Ethical considerations of community-based participatory research: Contextual underpinnings for developing countries. *International Journal of Preventive Medicine, 5*(10), 1328–1336.

Ji, E. G. (2006). A study of the structural risk factors of homelessness in 52 metropolitan areas in the United States. *International Social Work, 49*(1), 107–117.

Knight, R. (2024). The causes all time high chronic homelessness: A panel analysis. *Empirical Economic Bulletin, An Undergraduate Journal, 17*(1), 12.

Lee, K., Cassidy, J., Mitchell, J., Jones, S., & Jang, S. W. (2023). Documented barriers to health care access among Latinx older adults: A scoping review. *Educational Gerontology, 49*(2), 81–95.

Liebenberg, L. (2022). Photovoice and being intentional about empowerment. *Health Promotion Practice, 23*(2), 267–273.

Lorenz, L., & Bush, E. (2022). Critical and creative thinking and Photovoice: Strategies for strengthening participation and inclusion. *Health Promotion Practice, 23*(2), 274–280.

Magaña, D. (2020). Local voices on health care communication issues and insights on Latino cultural constructs. *Hispanic Journal of Behavioral Sciences, 42*(3), 300–323.

Manzano-Sanchez, H., Matarrita-Cascante, D., & Outley, C. (2019). Barriers and supports to college aspiration among Latinx high school students. *Journal of Youth Development, 14*(2), 25–45.

Moya, E. M., Chavez-Baray, S. M., Loweree, J., Mattera, B., & Martinez, N. (2017). Adults experiencing homelessness in the U.S.–Mexico Border region: A Photovoice project. *Frontiers in Public Health, 5*, 113.

Ogunnusi, M. (2019). Photovoice: A focus on dialogue, young people, peace and change. *Journal of Dialogue Studies, 7*.

Rana, D. K. (2024). *Quality Education for Underrepresented Groups: Bridging the Gap.*

Reckitt. (2018, February 20). *Manisha's Photovoice Project* [Video]. YouTube. https://www.youtube.com/watch?v=Voh7MMsR_Bo

Rodriguez, N. M., Martinez, R. G., Ziolkowski, R., Tolliver, C., Young, H., & Ruiz, Y. (2022). "COVID knocked me straight into the dirt": Perspectives from people experiencing homelessness on the impacts of the COVID-19 pandemic. *BMC Public Health* 22, no. 1: 1327.

Valdez, L. A., Jaeger, E. C., Garcia, D. O., & Griffith, D. M. (2023). Breaking down machismo: Shifting definitions and embodiments of Latino manhood in middle-aged Latino men. *American Journal of Men's Health, 17*(5), 15579883231195118.

Valenzuela, A., Garcia, E., Romo, H., & Perez, B. (2012). Institutional and structural barriers to Latino/a achievement. *Association of Mexican American Educators Journal, 6*(3).

Walls, J., & Holquist, S. E. (2019). Through their eyes, in their words: Using photo-elicitation to amplify student voice in policy and school improvement research. *Research Methods for Social Justice and Equity in Education*, 151–161.

Wang, C. C. (1999). Photovoice: A participatory action research strategy applied to women's health. *Journal of Women's Health, 8*(2), 185–192.

Wang, C. C., Yi, W. K., Tao, Z. W., & Carovano, K. (1998). Photovoice as a participatory health promotion strategy. *Health Promotion International, 13*(1), 75–86.

Watershed Productions. (n.d.). *Voices from the margins*. https://www.watershedproductions.ca/project/voices-from-the-margins-watershed-productions/

CHAPTER SEVEN

Échale Ganas:
Exploring the Support Systems of Latinx Early Educators in Teacher Education Programs

Aura Pérez-González

Introduction

ACCORDING TO THE U.S. Census Bureau (2020), people who identify as Hispanic or Latinx[1] are now the second largest racial and ethnic group in the United States, constituting over 18% of the total U.S. population. However, despite the prominence of Latinx people in the United States, there is a systemic scarcity of teachers of Color, including Latinx teachers in the United States (Gershenson et al., 2021; Haddix, 2017; Sandles Jr, 2020; Souto-Manning & Cheruvu, 2016; Villegas et al., 2012). Teachers who identify as white account for more than 83% of the U.S. K-12 teaching force; in contrast, only 9% of the teaching force identifies as Latinx (National Center for Education Statistics [NCES], 2021; Sleeter, 2017; Souto-Manning & Cheruvu, 2016). Similarly, there is also a lack of Latinx teachers within the field of early childhood education (ECE), in which 65% of teachers identify as white non-Hispanic, and 15% identify as Latinx (Paschall et al., 2020).

To better understand the pervasive lack of Latinx teachers within the U.S. educational system, it is important to recognize the systemic historical exclusion, dismissal, and racially biased policies that have prevented people of Color, from teacher education programs, and the teaching profession (Bettini et al., 2022, Fultz, 2004; Siddle Walker, 2015). To tackle the systemic exclusion of teachers of Color, scholars have focused on the importance of increasing the number of teachers of Color by highlighting the positive social, emotional, and academic influence that teachers of Color have on *all* students (Bettini et al., 2022; Gershenson et al., 2017; Kesner, 2000; Redding, 2019). Moreover, given the recent increase of young Latinx students in the United States (Egalite et al., 2015; Moll, 1988; Rasheed et al., 2020; Shirrell et al., 2023; Turner et al., 2013), researchers have also recommended the need for more Latinx teachers to reflect the racial and ethnic identities of young Latinx students in the United States. Consequently, the lack of racial and ethnic diversity in the field of early childhood education (Gillanders et al., 2021; Souto-Manning & Cheruvu, 2016; Whitebook et al., 2018) has spurred efforts to diversify the field and increase the recruitment of Latinx people into early childhood teacher education programs. However, missing from these recruitment efforts are the voices of Latinx people and *their* insights on what support systems and retention efforts they experienced during their early education teacher education programs.

The purpose of this research study was, therefore, to explore Latinx early childhood educators' reflections on their teacher education program experiences and trajectories. The research questions of this study were: (1) What do Latinx early educators believe contributed to their sustainment and retention in their teacher education programs? and (2) What and/or who supported their journey while in their early childhood teacher education programs (ECTEPs)?

Theoretical Framework

Given that all the participants of this study self-identified as Latinx, a LatCrit theoretical framework was engaged to focus on the racialized experiences of the Latinx early educator participants during their teacher education programs. A LatCrit theoretical framework was chosen for this study because it: (1) acknowledged the pervasiveness of race and racism within all facets of U.S. structures (law, economy, politics, language, education), and its impact on Latinx people, (2) recognized how race can intersect with other identities pertinent to Latinx people, such as immigration status, multilingualism, culture, ethnicity, and influence the entrenched U.S. structures that implicitly and/

or explicitly impact Latinx people (Chávez-Moreno, 2023; Huber, 2010, 2023; Solórzano & Yosso, 2001). Moreover, LatCrit enabled for multiple intersectional experiences to be emphasized to show "how multiple forms of oppression can intersect within the lives of people of Color and how those intersections manifest in our daily experiences to mediate our education" (Huber, 2010, p. 77). LatCrit was therefore employed to better understand the role that the participant's race, ethnicity, and intersectional identities played in the retention and support efforts they experienced during their early childhood teacher education programs.

Literature Review

Latinx People and the U.S. Educational System

Understanding the role of race in U.S. structures requires acknowledging the history of racism and the perpetuation of deficit-based paradigms (Valencia, 2019), cultural deficit models, and assimilationist policies that oppress people of Color. Racist ideologies are embedded in the U.S. educational system through biased standardized testing, low academic expectations for students of Color, and assimilationist practices (Ladson-Billings, 2001; Picower, 2009; Souto-Manning & Cheruvu, 2016; Souto-Manning & Price-Dennis, 2012). This has led to an educational debt owed to people of Color and the perpetuation of deficit-based narratives about their educational potential (Ladson-Billings, 2006). Latinx people are perceived as deficient due to low educational attainment and lack of enrollment in teacher education programs, which reflect systemic obstacles rather than their effort or intellectual capabilities (Gonzalez et al., 2021; Souto-Manning, 2013).

Structural barriers for Latinx students include underfunded, overenrolled, and racially segregated K-12 schools (Gonzalez et al., 2021; Valencia, 2019). Latinx students are least likely to enroll in preschool and receive culturally sustaining teaching and are more likely to be pushed out of high schools and face immigration-related barriers such as lack of financial aid and employment opportunities (Gonzalez et al., 2021).

Despite these barriers, over 21% of U.S. undergraduate students identify as Latinx, making them the second largest ethnic group in higher education. However, they are overrepresented in community colleges and underrepresented in 4-year institutions (Gillanders et al., 2021; Postsecondary National Policy Institute, 2023). Less than 14% of Latinx undergraduates in 4-year institutions pursue education degrees, despite the need for more teachers of Color (Carver-Thomas, 2018; Gonzalez et al., 2021). Only 15% of early childhood educators identify as Latinx (Paschall et al., 2020). Given these educational obstacles, it is crucial to explore the role of race in early childhood teacher education programs to understand the challenges Latinx early educators face.

Latinx People and Early Childhood Teacher Education Programs

Despite calls for a more racially and ethnically diverse teaching force, U.S. university-based teacher education programs are predominantly white, perpetuate whiteness, and conserve racist ideologies (Kohli et al., 2022, p. 53; Sleeter, 2001, 2017). Similarly, early childhood teacher education programs are largely staffed by white professors, field experience supervisors, mentor teachers, and students (Gillanders et al., 2021). ECTEPs are also strongly influenced by white European psychologists and developmental theorists that normed their findings on Eurocentric families and cultures (Cheruvu et al., 2015; Gillanders et al., 2021; Pérez & Saavedra, 2017). Therefore, the experiences that Latinx people encounter once they enroll in early childhood teacher education programs are extensions of the embedded racism that lives within the U.S. educational system as whole.

Contextualizing the educational landscape that Latinx early educators must navigate clarifies the embedded racism and deficit-based narratives that Latinx people experience within ECTEPs. There is therefore a need to center the voices and experiences of Latinx early childhood educators who have had to navigate such ECTEPs to inform ECTEPs on how to better support and retain Latinx teacher candidates and racially diversify the early childhood teaching workforce. The purpose of this study was therefore to explore the experiences and support systems of Latinx early educators and what they express as having contributed to their sustainment and retention in their ECTEPs.

Methodology

To explore the experiences and support systems of Latinx early educators during their ECTEPs, a qualitative FotoHistorias (or Photostories) methodology was utilized for this study. FotoHistorias fuses both PhotoVoice (Wang & Burris, 1994; Wang et al., 1996; Luo, 2017) and Photo Elicitation (Collier, 1957; Clark-Ibáñez, 2004; Rose, 2016) visual research methods, to employ both participatory and nonparticipatory approaches (Gomez, 2020). FotoHistorias empowers participants by centering their participant-generated photography (PhotoVoice) and conversations around such photographs (photo elicitation) during the research interview to facilitate in-depth discussions about their lived experiences (Gomez & Vannini, 2017). FotoHistorias was intentionally employed because it empowers participants to take an active role in the research process and leverages the rich and long tradition of storytelling present in the Latinx community (Gomez & Vannini, 2017).

Participants

Purposeful sampling (Merriam, 2009) was used to select participants using the following criteria: (1) Self-identified as Latinx, (2) taught in an early childhood education setting (serving ages birth through 8 years), (3) were students in the K-12 schooling system within the United States, and (4) had completed a teacher education program at an institution of higher education in the United States (earning a bachelor's degree or higher). Three early childhood educators participated in this study: Diego, Clara, and Valentina.

Table 7.1 *Participant demographics*

Name	Age	Place of birth	Education/ institution of higher education	Occupation	Years in ECE contexts	Ethnicity
Diego	33	Jalisco, Mexico	B.A. in Liberal Studies with a K-8 Bilingual Authorization and a Minor in science/ California State University (CSU)	Transitional Kindergarten - 1st Grade English Language Development Teacher	13	Mexican
Valentina	35	Los Angeles, CA, USA	Master's in Early Childhood Education / California State University (CSU)	Social Skills Coordinator/ Supporting Children w/Special Needs	11	Guatemalan
Clara	27	Los Angeles, CA, USA	Master's in Early Childhood Education/ California State University (CSU)	Quality Monitor for Early Head Start for Family Child Care Providers	5	Mexican & Salvadoran

Data Collection

The following methods were used to collect data: participatory photography, photo elicitation, and pláticas (casual conversational interviews) through Zoom (Fierros & Delgado Bernal, 2016; Gomez, 2020; Gomez & Vannini, 2017). Data were collected for 4 months, and each participant was engaged in a plática for a total of four times, with each plática averaging a total of 57 minutes. Pláticas were chosen because they differ from conventional interviews that are stringent on protocol and what the researcher can or cannot say. Instead, pláticas are meant to foster humanizing spaces where participants and researchers can bring their full authentic selves and not worry about the "cultural and general limitations of interview research methodologies" (Fierros & Delgado Bernal, 2016, p. 102). Therefore, the use of pláticas allowed the participants and researchers to engage in a culturally authentic and reciprocal conversation.

Furthermore, before each scheduled plática, each participant was invited to engage in participatory photography (Prins, 2010) by capturing or selecting a photograph that they felt represented what supported them and/or the ways in which they were sustained and retained during their ECTEPs trajectories. Afterward, during the pláticas, photo elicitation (Shaw, 2021) was used to trigger the beginning of the pláticas, to empower the participants to lead the plática, and to make space for participants to disclose what they felt was most pertinent to the study. Each participant shared at least one photograph each time they participated in a plática. The modalities of the photographs also varied by participant; some photos were printed, others were digital, or multiple photographs were compiled into a collage.

Data Analysis

The audio from each plática was recorded, transcribed, and analyzed using a reflexive thematic analysis approach (Braun & Clarke, 2022). Patterns within the data were coded (Saldaña, 2021) to develop overarching categories, which were then collapsed into themes. A LatCrit lens was employed during analysis, utilizing deductive codes related to the theoretical framework and research study, such as race, racism, identity, Latinx, motivation, support, and obstacles. Inductive codes also emerged, including immigrant, mentorship, family, financial hardship, first-generation, translanguaging, othered, and sacrifice. These codes were grouped into broader categories: family, faculty, and peer mentors. These categories were then collapsed into themes representing what supported, retained, and sustained the participants during their ECTEPs.

Findings and Discussion

The findings of the study established that the social emotional support, demystification of Insitutions of Higher Education (IHEs) and ECTEPs, and mentorship efforts provided by the participant's family, faculty, and peers are what supported, retained, and sustained the participants during their ECTEPs.

Latinx Families as Emotional Support

During the pláticas, families were the most frequently cited support system by all participants, reflecting the deeply ingrained value of education, collectivism, and family among the Latinx participants. Vasquez-Salgado et al. (2015) noted that while schooling emphasizes individual achievement, many immigrant groups, like those from Latin America, uphold strong collectivistic values, often centering on family collectivity. Each participant disclosed feeling a duty to their families, influencing their decision to enroll in ECTEPs close to home. For instance, Diego shared a picture of himself as an early educator in his classroom, emphasizing that he was able to become an educator because of his family's continuous support. He also shared how he felt a duty to his family led him to decide to attend an ECTEP close to his family's home. Diego stated:

Figure 7.1 *Diego teaching*

> Like I told you, being a first-generation college student, it was not only hard for me, but for my parents as well. So supporting each other. I mean, I'm very attached to my family. So I didn't really want to go far. Although I did get accepted to different locations, I said, well, this one's closest.

Attending teacher education programs close to home enabled the participants to maintain access to words of encouragement and emotional support. The findings align with studies showing that Latinx people emphasize familismo, a strong family focus and duty, with families being a primary source of emotional support for college students (Azpeitia & Bacio, 2022; Martinez, 2013).

Valentina also credited her family with supporting her educational trajectory as an early educator. She shared, "I definitely owe it to my parents. I don't know where I would be without their strong support system." During each plática, Valentina compiled photos into collages that visually depicted her responses. For example, in the collage below, Valentina included a picture of a Latino family to highlight her family as a crucial support system throughout her academic journey.

Figure 7.2 *Latino family*

Such findings align with Jabbar et al.'s (2019) work that detailed how Latinx families provide support through "pep talks" and "words of encouragement" to support Latinx students in perceiving themselves as capable of attaining academic degrees (p. 263). These findings highlight the important role that Latinx families play in supporting Latinx early educators during their teacher education programs. Even though Latinx families may not be familiar with the higher education system and even though they are rarely acknowledged by ECTEPs, they play an integral role in the support and retention of Latinx early childhood teacher candidates within teacher education programs.

Faculty and Staff Supporting the Demystifying of IHEs and ECTEPs

University faculty and staff were also found to be strong support systems for the Latinx participants throughout their teacher education programs. The participants credited faculty with helping them demystify how to navigate their IHEs and ECTEPs. For example, Diego shared how he intentionally cultivated faculty and staff mentorship relationships to form an academic network of support. During a plática, Diego also divulged that he kept in touch with many of his professors and counselors and still sought them out for advice. He also shared a picture (see Figure 7.3) of himself earning an award for teaching excellence, which he expressed was indicative of how his teaching has been enhanced because of his continued support from professors and counselors. Diego's recollections support the notion that faculty and staff play an important role in helping Latinx students navigate the hidden curriculum, policies, and bureaucracies of IHEs and ECTEPs.

Figure 7.3 *Diego's teaching excellence award*

During a different plática, Valentina recalled how her professor, Dr. Elizabeth, asked how to better support her during class given Valentina's hearing impairment. Dr. Elizabeth modified her teaching style by intentionally facing the front row during lectures to give Valentina better access and support her academic success. During the plática, Valentina also shared a picture of herself, exemplifying her confidence in taking selfies that show her hearing aid and feeling more comfortable discussing her hearing aid.

Figure 7.4 *Valentina's selfie*

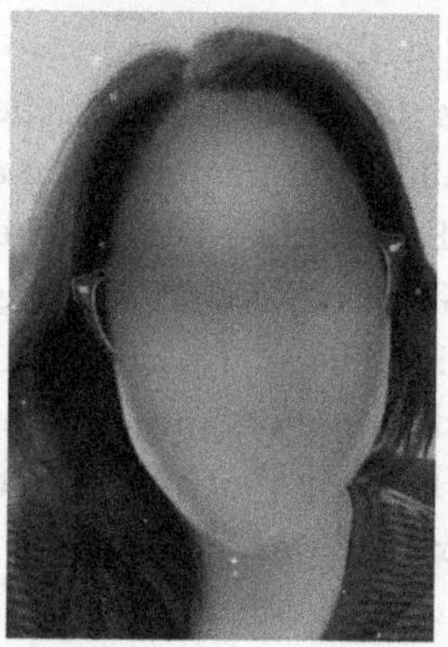

Valentina recalled sharing with her professor, "I think you are by far like the one professor who really cared about making sure that I'm hearing and grasping, you know, the concepts in school." Dr. Elizabeth's interest in making learning accessible to Valentina exemplifies how faculty have the power to remove issues of accessibility to Latinx students with disabilities who are navigating ECTEPs. The findings of this study align with research studies that have called for a more intentional study of the preparation and development of teacher educators to support high-quality teacher education programs and its students (Cochran-Smith, 2003; Cochran-Smith et al., 2020).

Peer Mentorship as Academic and Emotional Support

Peer mentorship was also a strong academic and emotional support system for the participants during their ECTEPs. For example, during a plática, Clara shared how a peer mentorship program supported her educational trajectory. The peer mentorship program paired Clara with a Latina peer mentor at a 4-year university that helped demystify the transfer process from community college to a 4-year university. Clara stressed how her mentor then motivated her to apply to a master's level ECTEP, even though Clara wasn't sure she was capable. Clara's mentor demystified the ECTEP by explaining what courses and continuously checking in throughout her educational trajectory. During a plática, Clara shared a picture of her master's graduation cap as evidence of what she was able to accomplish with the help of her peer mentor.

Figure 7.5 *Clara's master's graduation cap*

Clara's mentor exemplified how ECTEPs can leverage racial affinity-based peer mentorship programs to support Latinx early childhood teacher candidates. Clara detailed:

> Like, I know, I want to get my master's—it's always been in my head. But I was really scared because I've never known anyone personally, like only professors. She's [her mentor] like, oh, I know the perfect program.

Clara's positive experience with her Latina mentor signals the benefits of Latinx students connecting and mentoring each other. As Rios-Ellis et al. (2015)

argued, "peer mentorship programs can provide a pathway through which underserved Latino students can receive assistance from high achieving peers who have undergone similar contextual experiences and understand firsthand the educational barriers one must overcome to achieve academic success" (p. 37). Therefore, ECTEPs can support Latinx early childhood teacher candidates by providing spaces where Latinx peers can build community and connect with each other.

Implications

This study focuses on the experiences of Latinx early educators during their ECTEPs, highlighting support, sustainability, and retention. The findings can spark crucial discussions on supporting Latinx individuals and implications for teacher education programs, the education field, and Latinx communities.

First, the study shows that teacher education programs can improve recruitment and retention by creating equitable environments with continuous support systems. This includes decentering whiteness (Kohli et al., 2022) and establishing Latinx-specific spaces for discussing race, family, and cultural values (Solórzano et al., 2000; Yosso, 2005; Yosso et al., 2009). Recruitment and retention initiatives should provide continuous guidance on navigating higher education and offer holistic support, including academic, personal, social, emotional, and racial aspects.

Second, the study emphasizes the importance of acknowledging the racial, linguistic, and cultural assets of Latinx people. Participants often experienced self-doubt due to internalized deficit-based paradigms. The education field must dispel these myths, expose embedded racism, and foster connections with Latinx families to support students of all ages.

Lastly, the study underscores the need for education on race, the history of racialization in the United States, and the impact of identifying as Latinx. It highlights the need to disrupt internalized deficit-based ideologies and reaffirm Latinx individuals' self-images, potential, and contributions to U.S. society, despite facing racial discrimination.

Conclusion

The purpose of this study was to explore the support, sustainment, and retention efforts experienced by Latinx early educators during their teacher education programs. This study aimed to counter majoritarian narratives that Latinx people are incapable of academic achievement or becoming educators by showcasing the experiences of three Latinx early educators who successfully completed an ECTEP despite numerous barriers. The findings demonstrate that Latinx early childhood educators can complete ECTEPs when provided with adequate support, retention efforts, and mentorship. It is crucial for teacher education programs, the education field, and U.S. society to focus on the successes of Latinx people and learn from them.

The use of FotoHistorias has implications for future studies aiming to center Latinx voices and counter deficit-based paradigms. This methodology allowed participants to express their experiences in multimodal ways (through conversations, participatory photography, and photo elicitation). FotoHistorias promoted a culturally authentic approach that empowered Latinx participants to lead discussions, share representative photographs, address racial discrimination, and advocate for better support and retention in early childhood teacher education programs.

Endnote

[1] The term Latinx is used to disrupt gender binaries and Spanish colonization (DeGuzmán, 2017).

References

Azpeitia, J., & Bacio, G. A. (2022). "Dedicado a mi familia": The role of familismo on academic outcomes among Latinx college students. *Emerging Adulthood, 10*(4), 923–937.

Bettini, E., Cormier, C. J., Ragunathan, M., & Stark, K. (2022). Navigating the double bind: A systematic literature review of the experiences of novice teachers of color in K–12 schools. *Review of Educational Research, 92*(4), 495–542. https://doi.org/10.3102/00346543211060873

Braun, V., & Clarke, V. (2022). *Thematic analysis: A practical guide*. SAGE Publications.

Carver-Thomas, D. (2018). Diversifying the teaching profession: How to recruit and retain teachers of Color. Learning Policy Institute. https://learningpolicyinstitute.org/sites/default/files/product-files/Diversifying_Teaching_Profession_REPORT_0.pdf

Chávez-Moreno, L. C. (2023). Examining race in LatCrit: A systematic review of Latinx critical race theory in education. *Review of Educational Research, 94*(4), 501–538.

Cheruvu, R., Souto-Manning, M., Lencl, T., & Chin-Calubaquib, M. (2015). Race, isolation, and exclusion: What early childhood teacher educators need to know about the experiences of pre-service teachers of Color. *The Urban Review, 47*(2), 237–265. doi:10.1007/s11256-014-0291-8

Clark-Ibáñez, M. (2004). Framing the social world with photo-elicitation interviews. *American Behavioral Scientist, 47*(12), 1507–1527. https://doi.org/10.1177/0002764204266236

Cochran-Smith, M. (2003). Learning and unlearning: The education of teacher educators. *Teaching and Teacher Education International Journal of Scholarship and Studies, 19*(1), 5–28. doi:10.1016/S0742-051X(02)00091-4

Cochran-Smith, M., Grudnoff, L., Orland-Barak, L., & Smith, K. (2020). Educating teacher educators: International perspectives. *The New Educator, 16*(1), 5–24.

Collier, J. (1957). Photography in anthropology: A report on two experiments. *American Anthropologist, 59*(5), 843–859.

DeGuzmán, M. (2017). Latinx: ¡Estamos aquí!, or being "Latinx" at UNC-Chapel Hill. *Cultural Dynamics, 29*(3), 214-230. https://doi.org/10.1177/0921374017727852

Egalite, A. J., Kisida, B., & Winters, M. A. (2015). Representation in the classroom: The effect of own-race teachers on student achievement. *Economics of Education Review, 45*, 44–52.

Fierros, C., & Delgado Bernal, D. (2016). Vamos a platicar: The contours of pláticas as Chicana Latina feminist methodology. Chicana/Latina Studies. *The Journal of Mujeres Activas en Letras y Cambio Social, 25*(2), 98–121.

Fultz, M. (2004). The displacement of Black educators post-Brown: An overview and analysis. *History of Education Quarterly, 44*(1), 11–45. https://doi.org/10.1108/JME-04-2017-0025

Gershenson, S., Hansen, M. J., & Lindsay, C. A. (2021). Teacher diversity and student success: Why racial representation matters in the classroom (Vol. 8). Harvard Education Press.

Gillanders, C., Riojas-Cortez, M., Laser, A., Miller, C., & Rudman, N. (2021). Preparing Latinx early childhood educators. *Journal of Early Childhood Teacher Education, 42*(4), 404–422.

Gomez, R. (2020). Photostories: a participatory photo elicitation visual research method in information science. *Qualitative and Quantitative Methods in Libraries. 9*(1), ISAST.

Gomez, R., & Vannini, S. (2017). Notions of home and sense of belonging in the context of migration in a journey through participatory photography. *The Electronic Journal of Information Systems in Developing Countries, 78*(1), 1–46.

Gonzalez, L. C., Ramirez, B. R., Burciaga, R., Huber, L. P., & Solorzano, D. G. (2021). Latino educational (in) opportunities: Causes, consequences, and challenges to unequal opportunities to learn. *In Handbook of Latinos and Education* (pp. 383–400). Routledge.

Haddix, M. M. (2017). Diversifying teaching and teacher education: Beyond rhetoric and toward real change. *Journal of Literacy Research, 49*(1), 141–149.

Huber, L. P. (2010). Using Latina/o critical race theory and racist nativism to explore intersectionality in the educational experiences of undocumented Chicana college students. *Educational Foundations, 24*, 77–96.

Huber, L. P. (2023). *Using Latina/o critical race theory (LatCrit) and racist nativism to explore intersectionality in the educational experiences of undocumented Chicana college students.* Educational Foundations.

Jabbar, H., Serrata, C., Epstein, E., & Sánchez, J. (2019). "Échale ganas": Family support of Latino/a community college students' transfer to four-year universities. *Journal of Latinos and Education, 18*(3), 258-276.

Kesner, J. E. (2000). Teacher characteristics and the quality of child-teacher relationships. *Journal of School Psychology, 38*(2), 133–149.

Kohli, R., Dover, A. G., Jayakumar, U. M., Lee, D., Henning, N., Comeaux, E., Nevárez, A., Hipolito, E., Carreno Cortez, A., & Vizcarra, M. (2022). Toward a healthy racial climate: Systemically centering the well-being of teacher candidates of color. *Journal of Teacher Education, 73*(1), 52–65. https://doi.org/10.1177/00224871211051980

Ladson-Billings, G. (2001). *Crossing over to Canaan: The journey of new teachers in diverse classrooms* (1st ed.). Jossey-Bass.

Ladson-Billings, G. (2006). From the achievement gap to the education debt: Understanding achievement in U.S. schools. *Educational Researcher, 35*(7), 3–12.

Luo, L. (2017). Photovoice: A creative method to engage library user community. *Library Hi Tech, 35*(1), 179–185.

Martinez, M. A. (2013). (Re) considering the role familismo plays in Latina/o high school students' college choices. *The High School Journal, 97*(1), 21-40.

Merriam, S. B. (2009). *Qualitative research: A guide to design and implementation.* Jossey-Bass.

Moll, L. C. (1988). Some key issues in teaching Latino students. *Language Arts, 65*(5), 465–472.

National Center for Education Statistics (NCES). (2021). *Characteristics of 2020–21 Public and Private K–12 School Teachers in the United States.* https://nces.ed.gov/pubs2022/2022113.pdf

Paschall, K., Madill, R., & Halle, T. (2020). Professional characteristics of the early care and education workforce: Descriptions by race, ethnicity, languages spoken, and nativity status. *OPRE Research Report #2020-107.* https://www.acf.hhs.gov/sites/default/files/documents/opre/professional-characteristics-ECE-dec-2020.pdf

Pérez, M. S., & Saavedra, C. M. (2017). A call for onto-epistemological diversity in early childhood education and care: Centering global south conceptualizations of childhood/s. *Review of Research in Education, 41*(1), 1–29. doi:10.3102/0091732X16688621

Picower, B. (2009). The unexamined whiteness of teaching: How white teachers maintain and enact dominant racial ideologies. *Racial Ethnicity and Education, 12*(2), 197–215.

Postsecondary National Policy Institute. (2023). Latino students. Fact Sheets. https://pnpi.org/factsheets/latino-students/

Prins, E. (2010). Participatory photography: A tool for empowerment or surveillance? *Action Research (London, England), 8*(4), 426–443. https://doi.org/10.1177/1476750310374502

Rasheed, D. S., Brown, J. L., Doyle, S. L., & Jennings, P. A. (2020). The effect of teacher–child race/ethnicity matching and classroom diversity on children's socioemotional and academic skills. *Child Development, 91*(3), e597–e618.

Redding, C. (2019). A teacher like me: A review of the effect of student–teacher racial/ethnic matching on teacher perceptions of students and student academic and behavioral outcomes. *Review of Educational Research, 89*(4), 499–535. https://doi.org/10.3102/0034654319853545

Rios-Ellis, B., Rascón, M., Galvez, G., Inzunza-Franco, G., Bellamy, L., & Torres, A. (2015). Creating a model of Latino peer education: Weaving cultural capital into the fabric of academic services in an urban university setting. *Education and Urban Society, 47*(1), 33-55.

Rose, G. (2016). Visual methodologies: An introduction to the interpretation of visual materials (4th ed). SAGE Publications.

Saldaña, J. (2021). The coding manual for qualitative researchers (4th ed). SAGE Publications.

Sandles Jr, D. (2020). Using critical race theory to explore the Black men teacher shortage. *Journal of Negro Education, 89*(1), 67–81.

Shaw, P. A. (2021). Photo-elicitation and photo-voice: Using visual methodological tools to engage with younger children's voices about inclusion in education. *International Journal of Research & Method in Education, 44*(4), 337–351. https://doi.org/10.1080/1743727X.2020.1755248

Shirrell, M., Bristol, T. J., & Britton, T. A. (2023). The effects of student–teacher ethnoracial matching on exclusionary discipline for Asian American, Black, and Latinx students: Evidence from New York City. *Educational Evaluation and Policy Analysis, 46*(3), 555–580. https://doi.org/10.3102/01623737231175461

Siddle Walker, V. (2015). School "outer-gration" and" tokenism": Segregated Black educators critique the promise of education reform in the Civil Rights Act of 1964. *Journal of Negro Education, 84*(2), 111–124. https://doi.org/10.7709/jnegroeduca-tion.84.2.0111

Sleeter, C. E. (2001). Preparing teachers for culturally diverse schools: Research and the overwhelming presence of whiteness. *Journal of Teacher Education, 52*(2), 94–106

Sleeter, C. E. (2017). Critical race theory and the whiteness of teacher education. *Urban Education, 52*(2), 155–169.

Solórzano, D. G., Ceja, M., & Yosso, T. J. (2000). Critical race theory, racial microaggressions, and campus racial climate: The experience of African American college students. *Journal of Negro Education, 69*(1), 60–73.

Solórzano, D. G., & Yosso, T. J. (2001). Critical race and LatCrit theory and method: Counter-storytelling. *Qualitative Studies in Education, 14*(4), 471–495.

Souto-Manning, M. (2013). Teaching young children from immigrant and diverse families. *Young Children, 68*(4), 72–80.

Souto-Manning, M., & Cheruvu, R. (2016). Challenging and appropriating discourses of power: Listening to and learning from early career early childhood teachers of Color. *Equity and Excellence in Education, 49*(1), 9–26.

Souto-Manning, M., & Price-Dennis, D. (2012). Critically redefining and repositioning media texts in early childhood teacher education: What if? And why? *Journal of Early Childhood Teacher Education, 33*(4), 304–321.

Turner, E. E., Dominguez, H., Empson, S., & Maldonado, L. A. (2013). Latino/a bilinguals and their teachers developing a shared communicative space. *Educational Studies in Mathematics, 84*(3), 349–370.

U.S. Census Bureau. (2020). 2020 U.S. population more racially and ethnically diverse than measured in 2010 [Data file]. https://www.census.gov/library/stories/2021/08/2020-united-states-population-more-racially-ethnically-diverse-than-2010.html

Valencia, R. (2019). *International deficit thinking: Educational thought and practice.* Routledge.

Vasquez-Salgado, Y., Greenfield, P. M., & Burgos-Cienfuegos, R. (2015). Exploring home-school value conflicts: Implications for academic achievement and well-being among Latino first-generation college students. *Journal of Adolescent Research, 30*(3), 271–305.

Villegas, A. M., Strom, K., & Lucas, T. (2012). Closing the racial/ethnic gap between students of Color and their teachers: An elusive goal. *Equity and Excellence in Education, 45*(2), 283–301.

Wang, C., & Burris, M. A. (1994). Empowerment through photo novella: Portraits of participation. *Health Education Quarterly, 21*(2), 171–186.

Wang, C., Burris, M. A., & Ping, X. Y. (1996). Chinese village women as visual anthropologists: A participatory approach to reaching policymakers. *Social Science & Medicine, 42*(10), 1391–1400. https://doi.org/10.1016/0277-9536(95)00287-1

Whitebook, M., McLean, C., Austin, L. J., & Edwards, B. (2018). Early childhood workforce index 2018. *Center for the study of childcare employment*, University of California at Berkeley.

Yosso, T. J. (2005). Whose cultural capital? A critical race theory discussion of community cultural wealth. *Race, Ethnicity, and Education, 8*(1), 69–91.

Yosso, T. J., Smith, W., Ceja, M., & Solórzano, D. (2009). Critical race theory, racial microaggressions, and campus racial climate for Latina/o undergraduates. *Harvard Educational Review, 79*(4), 659–691.

Chapter Eight

PhotoVoice: Possibilities and Hope for Course Evaluation and Student Critical Reflection

Carolyn Brennan, Kristen French, Meilan Jin, Adilene Landa, Charlene Montaño Nolan, and Margarita Ruiz Guerrero

Illuminate the space with wonder and awe.
Breathe in notes of truth and joy.
Tied together, work on the flaw.
You're capable hoy.

This photograph and poem—created in the context of a student reflecting upon a course they just completed—invites much speculation. What might the clever interplay of light, shadows, symbols, natural materials, and language suggest about the student? About the faculty instructor? The course content? What might we learn about our pedagogy by thinking with the visual and textual information crafted by the student?

In this reflection, we take up these sensemaking stances to articulate the possibility of PhotoVoice as an anticolonial method for co-constructing knowledge about student experiences and teaching effectiveness. This work is situated as critique and re-crafting of the 50 years of student evaluations of teaching (SETs) in institutions of higher education and the body of literature that critiques their validity, reliability, and bias (e.g., Beecham, 2009; Boring et al., 2016; Braga et al., 2014; Hoefer et al., 2012). The literature is clear that these assessments more accurately capture student bias than effective teaching (Boring et al., 2016) and fail women, faculty of color, faculty with accents, and other groups who are systematically rated lower than those with dominant identities, even when other variables are controlled (Chávez & Mitchell, 2020; Wallace et al., 2019). Indeed, our own "theories of the flesh" (Moraga, 1981, 2021) bear these findings with numerous examples of student ratings more focused on the appeal of our personhood and apparent usefulness of our content than the transformative nature of our pedagogies.

This chapter is a speculative work grounded in our efforts to craft a process of understanding whether and how our teaching is embraced by our students. Adhering to the anticolonial theories that guide our work and ways of being, and honoring PhotoVoice as a tool of disruption, we engage in a more aesthetic approach to knowledge sharing than the dominant research paper enables. Inspired by Kristen's work as an Indigenous Craftivist—whose cooking, landscaping, traditional beading, foraging, and candle making each contribute to a more just and beautiful world—we reject the notion that literature, data, methods, and results must be presented as linear and separate components. Instead, we use these elements as crafting materials to create something more complete and reflective of our work.

We begin with a grounding of our context, relationships, and process of gathering data, which includes Adilene's PhotoVoice and poem, transcripts of our recorded interviews with Adilene and Kristen, and notes from our many research conversations. We then use what we are referring to as "crafting materials" to construct meaning from/with our data and one another. These are organized into three sections (1) PhotoVoice (both a broad overview and the specific assignment informing this work), (2) anticolonial theories, and (3) matrices of power (Collins, 2000) that offer insights into the possibility of PhotoVoice for course evaluations and student reflections. We close with our enduring learnings that emerged during this process and implications for PhotoVoice as an anticolonial tool.

Crafting Context

We write this reflection as a group of faculty and a teacher candidate at a college of education located on the traditional homelands of Coast Salish Peoples. The five faculty members call ourselves the DEJJA VU Collective and we stand for Diversity, Equity, Justice, Joy, and Action, Values Understanding. We came together to hold one another in loving care within our professional institution to envision and enact radical change. After nearly a year of what de Oliveira Andreotti and colleagues (2015) refer to as "antagonistic conflict" (investment in the system as is), we sought other modes of existence with our students' "agonistic conflict" (reinvesting our ingenuity in plural forms of knowledge making), particularly drawing on critical and anticolonial theories and methodologies (Archibald et al., 2022; Collins, 2008; de Oliveira Andreotti et al., 2015; Grande, 2018; Tuck & Yang, 2018; Tuck & Yang, 2023). Specifically, we utilized PhotoVoice as a tool to elicit students' multivoiced and multimodal reflections at the closure of our courses. Adilene (teacher candidate) joined our Collective to co-author this piece with us after completing Kristen's course and expressing eagerness to conduct research and writing. Thus, while content analysis of the full data set of course evaluations is underway, this chapter is focused on examining the possibilities and limitations of PhotoVoice from multiple perspectives (teacher, student, researcher, crafter).

To create this story we drew on the praxis of collective autoethnography (Karalis Noel et al., 2023) and "Betweener autoethnographies" (Diversi & Moreira, 2018). "Betweener autoethnographies" includes writing and researching by "making the personal political, talking back to the oppressors' version of history—for survival within the dominant patriarchal White supremacist Western ideology" (Diversi & Moreira, 2018, p. 15). Collective autoethnography provided our methodological tools to "co-construct narratives in a communal context" (Karalis Noel et al., 2023, p. 1). Our goal was to deconstruct the binary between student and teacher as opposing viewpoints and instead put these valences into conversation to create a more holistic and relational process of research and product that represents our myriad interpretations that are layered throughout the remainder of this piece.

Specifically, the DEJJA VU Collective met regularly to design the PhotoVoice evaluation and discuss possible interpretations and questions arising from

Adilene's poem and imagery. We took research notes during these meetings, which became analytic notes during the sensemaking process. This included collaborative data collection and interviewing, group meaning making of data, and collaborative co-narration through our writing. Margarita, Meilan, Charlene, and Carrie conducted a semi-structured interview with Adilene and Kristen to better understand context and personal meaning. This interview was recorded and transcribed. Our meanings and intentions emerged in conversation and collective authoring of this piece.

Crafting Materials

We frame our learnings in this process in relation to what we are calling "the crafting materials"—the interplay of methodologies (frameworks) and methods (practices) that anchor our collective knowledge building and speak to broader possibilities for PhotoVoice beyond this one experience. These "crafting materials" are tightly braided, yet for pedagogical purposes we unwind them.

These braids provide structure for the betweener and collective autoethnography that follows. The conversations between theory, data, and our sensemaking are expressed in various ways: sometimes as direct quotes from transcripts or research notes, and at other times as paraphrases combining several data points. We use our names in italics to reflect the voices from which these sensibilities unfolded in our conversations.

Material 1. PhotoVoice

We employed PhotoVoice as Wang and Burris (1997) suggest, as both a methodology and method. As a methodology, PhotoVoice is based on the ideas of documentary photography, feminist research theory, and Freirean empowerment that seek to promote social change from within oppressed communities (Langdon et al., 2014; Strack et al., 2004). These principles promote participant involvement and engagement and allow for the exploration of often hidden realities. We build on the work of scholar-activists who use PhotoVoice to document students' experiences with course content (Chio & Fandt, 2007; Langdon et al., 2014; Pérez et al., 2016; Ruiz Guerrero & Brennan, 2023). "PhotoVoice can incorporate voices often left out of academic and policy dialogues: members of disadvantaged and socially marginalized communities" (Mejia et al., 2013, p. 302).

What follows is our understanding of how the multimodal, aesthetic qualities of PhotoVoice created a generative space for Adilene to consider what she learned, what she will bring with her into her new role as a teacher, and all in relation to "pieces" of her identity that she described as salient in this course. Again, we use transcript and meeting notes to recraft this narrative.

Kristen: Adilene created the photograph and poem at the conclusion of a newly developed course, *Seminar in Racial Justice Praxis,* developed and taught by Kristen, for all elementary education students. The course is offered in the context of their internship in primary grade classrooms to help them work toward dismantling injustice, oppression, and unsettling settler-colonialism in U.S. schooling through community partnerships, pedagogy, and action. The goals, outcomes, and enduring understandings seek to cultivate an ethical community space, re-center community consciousness, enact pedagogies of unsettling settler colonialism, dismantle injustice and oppression, and focus on truth-telling, healing, joy, and action. Kristen taught with Goldy Muhammad's *Unearthing Joy* (2023) and Bettina Love's *We Want To Do More Than Survive* (2019) and asked students to critically engage with Yolanda Sealy-Ruiz's (2022) praxis of the "Archeology of Self [1]—a deep excavation and exploration of beliefs, biases, and ideas that shape who we engage in our work" (p. 22). This racial literacy model includes interruption, historical literacy, and critical reflection, humility, and love.

Building on these course foundations, each teacher candidate chose a critical friends seminar group to put theory into practice. Adilene created a candle in her radical joy and racial healing collective (which Meilan, Margarita, Carrie, and Charlene later learned is the same candle that illuminated her PhotoVoice). Together with her colleagues she engaged in relationship building through textual analysis of *The Racial Healing Handbook* (Singh, 2019), craftivism (e.g., candle making and beading), and critical dialogue.

A central tenet of Kristen's course is the "pursuit of joy" (Muhammad, 2023, p. 17). Gholdy Muhammad grounds "joy" as the ultimate goal of culturally and historically responsive teaching and learning (p. 17). Centering the "pursuit of joy ... [helps] students to uplift beauty, aesthetics, truth, ease, wonder, wellness, solutions to the problems of the world, and personal fulfillment" (p. 17). When you see "joy" in the following narratives, know that it is rooted in course content, pedagogy, and our scholarship.

Everyone: For those of us who have taught courses that challenge hegemonic beliefs about the "goodness" of schooling, particularly for minoritized children and their communities, we have come to expect and accept course evaluations that reflect students' axiological (value-laden) and epistemological claims about the worthiness (or lack thereof) of our content in their future teaching or the ontological claims about our abilities as instructors to impart knowledge. As Kristen put it, "They [student evaluations of teaching] give me anxiety." Even the most complimentary of evaluation ratings or comments often leave us wondering of our candidates, "how has this course influenced the kind of teacher you are learning to be?"

Kristen: It was with a great deal of "let's see what happens" that Kristen prompted students:

> "Please create/choose a photo, image, symbol, or art/craft to reflect your explorations/experiences/takeaways, etc ... from racial justice praxis and/or this course. Please consider the [College's] vision as a framework for grounding your reflections, but do not feel limited by this vision. Ultimately, this reflection is for you to take with you long after you leave this course."

Kristen hoped to learn how students were connecting to or developing comprehensive frameworks around the enduring understandings of the course, and potentially applying them to practice.

Everyone: Perhaps because we have come to expect and accept the anxiety that comes with SETs, the collective refrain when interpreting Adilene's piece became, "What a gift!" Even without knowing the full context, or even who Adilene was, is, and is becoming, we all saw aspects of our hopes and dreams for future teachers embedded in her coupling of image and text.

Adilene: "... what I got out from creating this image and poem was definitely joy, more creativity. I got a space and time to be thoughtful and curious in the sense of how I wanted to create both the poem and how I wanted to incorporate what I had learned throughout the whole quarter. I was able to kind of mix some of the options together with having, like a piece of craft that we had created with our joy group, and then capturing it with photography, which I am also fond of, and then tying it together with poetry, which I also, like, value and love … And so I believe it made it really meaningful. And so that is why I almost felt as if I was giving pieces of myself, and so, therefore it's like creating a tie in which I then bring forth with myself."

Material 2. Anticolonial (Re)Makings and Analysis

Settler-coloniality is a violence and structure—it is an ongoing mechanism of logic and action that severs a person from their personhood to justify exploitative relations (e.g., slavery) while simultaneously removing peoples from their lands and waters (e.g., Indigenous physical and cultural genocide) in explicit efforts to remake land into property and maintain hierarchical relations to power (Tuck & McKenzie, 2015). All U.S. universities are on Indigenous land; therefore, higher education is a project of settler colonialism to "erase" Indigenous and existing knowledges and "replace" with Eurocentric epistemologies and practices (Patel, 2016, p. 38). A scoping review of decolonial and anticolonial theory are beyond this chapter, but we unpack two tenets central to the anticolonial possibilities of PhotoVoice in course evaluation processes.

Settler-colonial logics—and resulting actions—are premised on the (erroneous, to our sensibilities) ideas of universality, singularity, and supremacy of knowledge (Mignolo, 2007; Deloria Jr., 2002). In the arena of knowledge production, to which teacher education holds a uniquely precarious relation, this facet of settler-colonial violence frames the very nature of what knowledge is (truth), how one goes about garnering knowledge (individual merit), and who may be knowledgeable (superior intellects). For student evaluations of teachers, this has meant students are tasked with assessing whether a teacher has correct knowledge and effectively conveyed this knowledge, which is tied to student perceptions of both the validity of the teachers' knowledge and reliability of the teacher to possess/convey this knowledge. In other words, SETs measure the capacity to which faculty can play by settler-coloniality's violent rules. And, our tenure and promotion processes, which require us to collect and submit SETs for evaluation, ensure we play, even as our institution claims a commitment to diversity, equity, and inclusion (DEI) and has taken up critical stances to put these ideals into practice, including the formation of DEI committees and initiatives across multiple levels (DEJJA VU Collective included).

Thus, using PhotoVoice as an alternative to standard SETs demands we hold an "ethic of incommensurability" (Tuck & Yang, 2018). Eve Tuck and K. Wayne Yang remind us that "incommensurability means that we cannot judge each other's justice projects by the same standard, but we can come to understand the gap between our viewpoints, and thus work together in contingent collaboration" (p. 2). There is a clear gap between the requirements of the higher ed institution to measure instructor's abilities (as defined by settler-colonial logics) and our sensibilities as anticolonial educators and scholars. This incommensurability is unlikely to dissipate with a new or revised SET, which poses a clear limitation to PhotoVoice as a possibility for course evaluations. Our ambition with PhotoVoice was, instead, to offer an alternative that unsettled settler-colonial metrics. In the context of an institution seeking to promote DEI initiatives, we find a "contingent collaboration" to reframe what it means to know whether/how our courses are transforming students' ideals, knowledge, and practices.

For Adilene, we saw her use PhotoVoice to challenge hegemonic epistemic frames in assessing Kristen's teaching quality and the interpersonal relations between knower and learner, which we unpack in greater detail our enduring learnings. Adilene's poem and picture revealed her ability to blend new information with her identity and prior knowledge, as evidenced by the combination of objects created in class with those from her home, and the blending of English with her native language. This piece provided insights into how Adilene is incorporating course content into her ways of knowing and being in a sustained way. We believe this approach effectively captures the impact of the course and instructor on student outcomes while resisting a reduction of her learning or Kristen's teaching into settler-colonial frames.

Material 3. Colonial Matrices of Domination

Patricia Hill Collins' framework, referred to as Matrix of Domination (2000, 2008) is our third crafting material, used to identify and challenge the interlocking dominations reproduced in uncritical evaluation methods. According to Collins (2008), there exists a dynamic, interactive matrix of domination that perpetuates systemic oppression in social institutions, including universities.

These include hegemonic (now referred to as cultural; Collins, 2008), interpersonal, structural, and disciplinary power dynamics. Hegemonic logics are those that justify the production of power relations between individuals, and individuals and institutions. In relation to settler-coloniality, the underlying cultural practices of SETs and normative interpretations of "quality teaching" perpetuate a system of epistemic dominance. As discussed in the previous section, those who look, think, and act most like academic norms are rated higher—regardless of the impact of their teaching on student learning. The logic becomes, **if** quantitative questions on SET are best teaching practices **and** the students rank these qualities highly, **then** the teacher must be good.

Interpersonal power relates to the everyday and accumulated experiences of individuals within social institutions. On their face, SETs may be an integral systemic reversal of traditional power dynamics (teachers in power) as students voice concerns or challenge these hierarchical relations. However, we argue that the ultimate nature of these power relations remains unchanged, simply the roles are reversed. Here the logic becomes, **if** your ways of being align with students' settler-colonial expectations, **then** you will earn high marks **and** you must be a good teacher.

Disciplinary power refers to the punishment doled out to those whose identities and knowledges stray too far from academic (read settler-colonial) standards. In this context, it is both the burden of carrying unjust criticisms and the use of SET scores to withhold tenure and promotion. **If** you do not align with institutional settler colonial expectations, **then** you must not be a good teacher **and** you should be punished.

Finally, structural power is the perceptively untouchable rights of the institution itself to enforce the other domains. Both history and hierarchy function to maintain the status quo- programs, departments, colleges, academic chairs, deans, and provosts all marching, with or without awareness, to the drum of **if** this is how it has always been done, **then** it is the way it should be done (regardless of whom it hurts).

In our review of Adilene's PhotoVoice reflection and our conversations, the aesthetic blending of image and words and the power of our multiple interpretations strengthened the bond between teacher and student rather than reinforcing divisive power dynamics. The following exchange between Kristen and Adilene illustrated this strengthened bond, demonstrating how it influenced Adilene to feel valued and cared for, and how she aspired to transform this experience in her future learning and as an educator

Kristen: "Receiving Adilene's PhotoVoice reflection, it was emotional. I do feel that there's an intimacy, a connection. I think I was amazed at the creativity and the depth. There was an embodiment of the course in this representation. It was a shared experience. So there was like this dialogic or this very connected reciprocal relationship going on. But I feel like it also went beyond just the head stuff and the academics. I don't even know how to describe what parts of you you put in there, but I received it, I felt it. I felt like I was able to see, you know, like, really see the image, that deeper content about who you are? It was about you. I feel like it was an authentic representation."

Adilene: "The experience of having courses where community building is really centered, I feel myself light up because it made me feel very valued and cared for and really joyful. The relationships alongside the content allowed me to take more of the learning with me where I head towards. And then thinking about what do I want to bring of myself in the future, as a future educator. What kind of impact do I want to do or create? It's how I make the course content and learning my own through my personalized expression. I think it was wonderful to be able to have an assignment like this and have this PhotoVoice very meaningful and impactful."

PhotoVoice can reframe the logic by resisting the division between teaching and learning and learning from learner(s). It challenges the hegemonic assumption that instructors merely transmit essential knowledge and skills to students. Learning occurs within the context of relationships, which are complicated in higher education by power dynamics that enable instructors to control content, delivery methods, and grading. This monolithic relationship is so prevalent that the importance of building relationships with students and its impact on their learning is often neglected (hooks, 1994). Adilene's poem reveals how relationships created a learning space where wonder and awe were nurtured, illuminating new knowledge construction.

Enduring Learnings

Through our betweener and collective autoethnography of the PhotoVoice

Course Reflection Assignment and interview with Adilene and Kristen, we learned that PhotoVoice radically (re)centered multimodal aesthetics, reflexivity, and relationality in the process of "course evaluation" for both Adilene and Kristen. We argue that these dynamics challenge hegemonic and interpersonal power relations and hold the potential to remake structural and disciplinary power matrices. We offer Figure 8.1 as an initial and imperfect visualization of our learnings and revealing the incommensurable limitations of this project to dismantle the system evaluation in higher ed. This figure was drafted during a conversation and details added and refined during the writing process. We find hooks (2000b) from the margin to the center a fruitful analogy to explain the complexity of this figure.

Figure 8.1

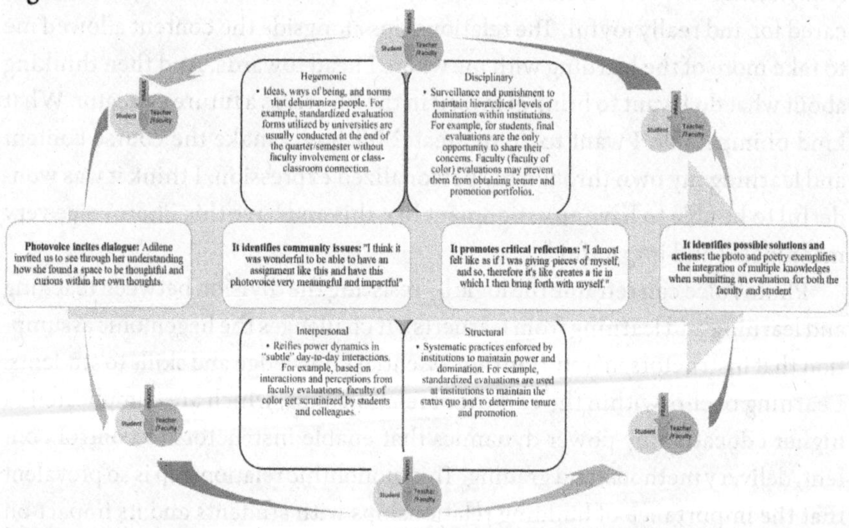

The edges represent critical thinking, resistance, praxis, and reflexivity. However, this critical work is not a separation between the margins and the center; rather, they are interconnected since each informs the other. As hooks (2000a) suggests, "[l]ove is an action ... it is useful to see love as a practice" (p. 165). With this in mind, we emphasize the arrows and circles at the margin as the space for loving transformation, where both students and teachers can thrive within praxis and reflexivity. These arrows and the praxis and reflexivity of students and teachers are at different "stages," signifying the importance of self-reflection, considering current realities, and potential changes as practical expressions of love.

At the center, we have the "problems" matrix of domination (Collins, 2008), which is identified to challenge these problems and to explore possibilities for negotiating and working towards transforming the encountered realities. These aspirations for transformation are supported by PhotoVoice and its purpose to interrupt, raise questions, and initiate dialogue within the community with the explicit intention to promote critical reflections, deconstruct such realities, and reconstruct them by prompting solutions.

Several crucial elements of the work within Kristen and Adilene's interactions are symbolized. Firstly, it emphasizes the importance of reciprocity in teaching and learning. Adilene and Kristen enacted teaching and learning reciprocity, they became supporters and co-conspirators (Hines & Ford, 2023). "Ultimately, say Kristen and Adilene, we empowered one another." Teaching and learning, in this context, are viewed as a mutual endeavor where both parties invest energy, time, and love. This reciprocal critical love is deeply rooted in an ethical commitment to caring for the communities in which teachers operate (Sealy-Ruiz, 2019). It embodies love as freedom, courage, "a bound to flourish" (hooks, 1994, p. 198), and transformative power for and from both.

Secondly, the figure emphasizes the continuous need for self-reflection when navigating power dynamics and oppressive systems. Kristen and Adilene's cyclical self-reflection, symbolized by the arrows, was a persistent, ongoing practice manifested throughout their interaction, including the faculty evaluation process. This self-reflective practice entails an ongoing examination of power structures, intersectionality, and privilege, while also exploring ways to foster a more just society.

Thirdly, the importance of amplifying the voices of those confronting oppressive circumstances, both presently and historically, is underscored. Adilene found a space to express her thoughts creatively through PhotoVoice, while Kristen utilized PhotoVoice to capture students' perspectives in the faculty evaluation process, fostering a more compassionate approach.

Lastly, PhotoVoice serves as a methodology that encourages praxis and reflexivity, enabling participants like Adilene and Kristen to challenge structural, hegemonic, disciplinary, and interpersonal barriers. Through their engagement with PhotoVoice, they work towards shifting power dynamics and dismantling oppressive realities faced by faculty members, especially those from marginalized backgrounds. Adilene's PhotoVoice serves as an engaging interruption, inviting participation in an aesthetic dialogue that identifies social issues, prompts critical reflections, and sparks opportunities for transformative change towards liberation (Carlson et al., 2006; Osseck et al., 2010; Strack et al., 2004; Wang & Burris, 1997).

A Project Unfinished

Leonardo da Vinci is quoted as saying, "Art is never finished, only abandoned." In the case of our craftings, we agree with the first half and commit to changing the second. Like a burning candle, our work evolves and shifts, casting new light on where we will go next. This includes potential restructuring of the PhotoVoice Assignment, which may, in future iterations, encourage students to include written interpretations of their art so that we can more accurately understand their perspectives in the absence of ongoing dialogue. Future instructions may also emphasize the opportunity for students to not only summarize their learning but also reflect on their experiences as learners throughout the course. We see the potential for this work to continue our collective resistance within the university and beyond.

References

Archibald, J. -A., Lee-Morgan, J., & De Santolo, J. (Eds.). (2022). *Decolonizing research: Indigenous storywork as methodology*. ZED Books Ltd.

Beecham, R. (2009). Teaching quality and student satisfaction: Nexus or simulacrum? *London Review of Education, 7*, 135–146. http://dx.doi.org/10.1080/14748460902990336

Boring, A., Ottoboni, K., & Stark, P. B. (2016). *Student evaluations of teaching (mostly) do not measure teaching effectiveness*. Science Open Research. doi:10.14293/S2199-1006.1.SOR-EDU.AETBZC.v1

Braga, M., Paccagnella, M., & Pellizzari, M. (2014). Evaluating students' evaluations of professors. *Economics of Education Review, 41*, 71–88. http://dx.doi.org/10.1016/j.econedurev.2014.04.002

Carlson, E. D., Engebretson, J., & Chamberlain, R. M. (2006). Photovoice as a social process of critical consciousness. *Qualitative Health Research, 16*, 6, 836–852.

Chávez, K., & Mitchell, K. M. W. (2020). Exploring bias in student evaluations: Gender, race, and ethnicity. *PS: Political Science & Politics, 53*(2), 270–274. doi:10.1017/S1049096519001744

Chio, V. C. M., & Fandt, P. M. (2007). Photovoice in the diversity classroom: Engagement, voice, and the "eye"/I of the camera. *Journal of Management Education, 31*(4), 484–504.

Collins, P. H. (2000, 2008). *Black feminist thought. Knowledge, consciousness, and the politics of empowerment.* Routledge Classics.

de Oliveira Andreotti, V., Stein, S., Ahenakew, C., & Hunt, D. (2015). Mapping interpretations of decolonization in the context of higher education. *Decolonization: Indigeneity, education & society, 4*(1), 21–40.

Deloria Jr, V. (2016). *Evolution, creationism, and other modern myths: A critical inquiry.* Fulcrum Publishing.

Diversi, M., & Moreira, C. (2018). *Betweener autoethnographies: A path towards social justice.* Routledge.

Grande, S. (2018). Refusing the university. In E. Tuck & K. W. Yang (Eds.), *Toward what justice? Describing diverse dreams of justice in education.* Routledge.

Hines, E. M., & Ford, D. Y. (2023). Educators as co-conspirators in decolonizing education for Black students. *Diverse Issues in Higher Education, 40*(17), 10–11.

Hoefer, P., Yurkiewicz, J., & Byrne, J. C. (2012). The association between students' evaluation of teaching and grades. *Decision Sciences Journal of Innovative Education, 10*, 447–459. do i:10.1111/j.1540-4609.2012.00345.

hooks, b. (1994). *Teaching to transgress: Education as the practice of freedom.* Routledge Press.

hooks, b. (2000a) *All about love.* HarperCollins Publishers Inc.

hooks, b. (2000b) *Feminist theorist: From margin to the center.* South End Press Classics.

Karalis Noel, T., Minematsu, A., & Bosca, N. (2023). Collective autoethnography as a transformative narrative methodology. *International Journal of Qualitative Methods, 22*, 1–9. https://doi.org/10.1177/16094069231203944

Langdon, J. L., Walker, A., Colquitt, G., & Pritchard, T. (2014). Using Photovoice to determine preservice teachers' preparedness to teach. *Journal of Physical Education, Recreation & Dance, 85*(1), 22–27.

Mejia, A. P., Quiroz, O., Morales, Y., Ponce, R., Chavez, G. L., & Torre, E. O. y. (2013). From madres to mujeristas: Latinas making change with Photovoice. *Action Research, 11*(4), 301–321. https://doi.org/10.1177/1476750313502553

Mignolo, W. D. (2007). Coloniality of power and de-colonial thinking-Introduction. *Cultural Studies, 21*(2-3), 155–167.

Moraga, C., & Anzaldúa, G. (1981). *This bridge called my back: Writings by radical women of color* (1st ed). Kitchen Table, Women of Color Press.

Moraga, C., & Anzaldúa, G. (2021). *This bridge called my back: Writings by radical women of color* (40th anniversary edition). SUNY Press.

Muhammad, G. (2023). *Unearthing joy: A guide to culturally and historically responsive teaching and learning.* Scholastic Inc.

Osseck, J., Hartman, A., & Cox, C. C. (2010). Photovoice: Addressing youths' concerns in a juvenile detention facility. *Children, Youth and Environments, 20*(2), 200–218.

Patel, L. (2016). *Decolonizing educational research: From ownership to answerability.* Routledge.

Pérez, M. S., Ruiz Guerrero, M. G., & Mora, E. (2016). Black feminist Photovoice: Fostering critical awareness of diverse families and communities in early childhood teacher education. *Journal of Early Childhood Teacher Education, 37*(1), 41–60.

Ruiz Guerrero, M. G., & Brennan, C. (2022). Using aesthetic approaches to meet and challenge the national standards: A both/and approach. In M. Nagasawa, B. B. Swadener, M. Bloch, & L. Peters (Eds.), *Transforming early years policy: A call to action.* Teachers College Press.

Sealey-Ruiz, Y. (September 5, 2019). *Education equity starts with critical love.* https://resilient-educator.com/classroom-resources/education-equity-starts-with-critical-love/

Sealey-Ruiz, Y. (2022). An archaeology of self for our times: Another talk to teachers. *English Journal, 111*(5), 21–26.

Singh, A. A. (2019). *The racial healing handbook: Practical activities to help you challenge privilege, confront systemic racism & engage in collective healing.* New Harbinger Publications, Inc.

Strack, R. W., Magill, C., & McDonagh, K. (2004). Engaging youth through Photovoice. *Health Promotion Practice, 5*(1), 49–58.

Tuck, E., & McKenzie, M. (2015). *Place in research: Theory, methodology, and methods.* Routledge.

Tuck, E., & Yang, K. W. (2018). *Toward what justice? Describing diverse dreams of justice in education.* Routledge.

Tuck, E., & Yang, K. W. (2023). Series editors introduction. In P. Mikulan & M. Zembylas (Eds.), *Working with theories of refusal and decolonization in higher education.* Routledge.

Wallace, S. L., Lewis, A. K., & Allen, M. D. (2019). The state of the literature on student evaluations of teaching and an exploratory analysis of written comments: Who benefits most? *College Teaching, 67*(1) 1–14.

Wang, C., & Burris, M. A. (1997). Photovoice: concept, methodology, and use for participatory needs assessment. *Health Education & Behavior, 24*(3), 369–387. doi: 10.1177/109019819702400309. PMID: 9158980.

Chapter Nine

Through the Eyes of Families:
Understandings of Community Through PhotoVoice

Betül Demiray Sandıraz

How do young children perceive their roles as civic agents to understand, participate in, and work for justice in a democratic society, and how are their understandings of community shaped? "Children's civic learning happens with or without our intentional participation" (Hauver, 2019, p. 17); in other words, their learning largely comes from interactions with parents/guardians, peers, and teachers. Understanding of community is vital for civic engagement, which is broadly defined as "how an active citizen participates in the life of a community in order to improve conditions for others or to help shape the community's future" (Adler & Goggin, 2005, p. 241). Young children are highly capable of civic engagement; however, scholarship on how it develops and is reinforced is limited, especially for children aged between 3 and 12 (Halvorsen, 2017; Koh, 2010). Additionally, we do not know enough about daily interactions of children and families that lead or do not lead to civic engagement. In this chapter, I share some major findings from a PhotoVoice project with international families living in the United States on their understanding of community and my reflections on the process of the PhotoVoice method.

This study is grounded in the frameworks of critical civic education for young children (Swalwell & Payne, 2019), bioecological model of human development (Bronfenbrenner & Morris, 2006), and the three-dimensional space of civic growth (Hauver, 2019) because they bring together three important elements of civic engagement: (1) critical perspective taking; (2) knowledge, skills, and motivation for action; and (3) interactions with people in direct and indirect ways.

PhotoVoice

Photovoice is a community-based participatory research method that encourages people to present their social and physical environment through photographs (Call-Cummings et al., 2019). Wang and Burris (1997) defined PhotoVoice as a "process by which people can identify, represent and enhance their community through a specific photographic technique" (p. 369). PhotoVoice stemmed from Freire's critical pedagogy, documentary photography, and feminist theory (Derr & Simons, 2019), and it has a potential to be a powerful tool for advocacy and social change in communities (Breny & McMorrow, 2021).

By its very nature, PhotoVoice serves as a method conducive to advancing efforts for social justice. However, employing PhotoVoice in a study does not guarantee having a social justice lens unless collaborators are intentional about this (Breny & McMorrow, 2021). It aims to enable reflections on a community and critical conversations among community members (Wang & Burris, 1997). Throughout a project, PhotoVoice may or may not reveal new information, yet it enables understanding a community and its strengths and problems from the perspectives of community members (Breny & McMorrow, 2021).

Photography training is sometimes included in PhotoVoice projects; however, it is not vital as long as collaborators know how to use the equipment because taking good pictures is not the goal. Instead, the stories and discussions revealed through the photographs are at the core (Breny & McMorrow, 2021). PhotoVoice has three major goals: (a) explore a community's strengths and concerns from the perspective of its members, (b) enable critical discussion and knowledge sharing through photographs in small and large groups, and (c) communicate with policy makers (Wang & Burris, 1997). However, every project may not reach the final step (Breny & McMorrow, 2021).

PhotoVoice and Children

PhotoVoice has been used in child-centered research across many disciplines, including anthropology, education, health, and sociology, and it is getting more popular (Volpe, 2019). The literature on PhotoVoice with children around the world shows the method is used in a variety of ways and for different purposes. This method is commonly employed to explore the understandings and experiences of children about a specific topic. For example, perspectives of children about rural schools in Spain (Raposo-Rivas et al., 2023), understandings and experiences of children about gender in home and school settings in the United States (Mackenzie & Talbott, 2018), understandings of community among kindergarteners in Canada (Alaca et al., 2016), climate conceptions among elementary graders in the United States (Herrick et al., 2022), perspectives of children on their school and communities in Sierra Leone (Samonova et al., 2022), and experiences of children living in orphanages in Kenya (Johnson, 2011) are some of the topics and issues researched through PhotoVoice.

PhotoVoice is also used as a tool for supporting creativity and incorporating art-based activities in early childhood settings in the United States (Gilbert, 2024), recovery-oriented self-assessment for children with behavioral disorders in Canada (Greco et al., 2017), identifying risky locations in school settings to prevent injuries in Japan (Oono et al., 2022), and documenting Native American children and their caregivers' perspectives of family and cultural strength in an intergenerational PhotoVoice project in the United States (Edwards et al., 2022).

Moreover, there are studies conducted with families with young children about their needs and experiences as new immigrants in Canada (Fakhari et al., 2023), mothers' experiences with parenting during the pandemic in Indonesia (Kiling et al., 2023), and family and community resilience from the perspectives of families with a history of adversity and resilience during the COVID-19 pandemic in Canada (Tan et al., 2024). The literature presents that PhotoVoice can be employed in various ways to reflect and discuss children's understandings and experiences from their own perspective, their caregivers' perspectives, or both. Because of its affordances, PhotoVoice with young children has a potential to be useful in research (Samonova et al., 2022). It is an innovative method to hear voices of children and collect data *with* them rather than data *from* them (Shaw, 2021).

Method

The underlying principles of PhotoVoice correspond with my conceptualization of civic engagement. Additionally, it is a child-friendly method that allows children to tell their stories in a unique and empowering way (Gallego et al., 2023). Thus, I collaborated with children ages 6 to 10 and their parents to conduct qualitative research employing PhotoVoice and to answer the following research question: What does community mean to international families, especially children moved from their home countries?

To collect data, I followed a three-step approach with three families between August 2023 and September 2023. First, I had a meeting with children and parents to inform them about the overall research project and discuss the principles of PhotoVoice. Each child got a handout explaining what they should do in this process. Second, children and parents practiced PhotoVoice based on the three questions that I shared with them in the information session and listed on the handout: (1) What does it mean to be a part of a community for me? (2) How can people make a difference in their community? (3) How do people in my family make a difference? During a 1- to 2-week period, both children and parents took 15 to 20 photographs to answer the three questions. Last, I interviewed each child and their parent together based on the photographs they took during the second step.

Collaborators

The project was conducted in an apartment complex on a Midwest U.S. university campus where most of the residents are international graduate students and their families. Therefore, the children and their parents were originally from different countries. I collaborated with three families, two from Kazakhstan and one from Indonesia. All children were elementary school aged, and at least one of their parents was pursuing a graduate degree. Below, I introduce each family by using pseudonyms.

The first family I interviewed is from Kazakhstan. Moldir (mother) and Birzhan (son) identify as Asian, Kazakh, and Muslim. They both speak Kazakh as their primary language and also use Russian and English at home. Birzhan is 10 years old and has two younger siblings. He qualifies for free or reduced-price lunch. While Moldir is a PhD student, the other parent is a physical education teacher and has a bachelor's degree.

The second family is from Indonesia. Edi (father) and Andi (daughter) identify as Asian, Indonesian, and Muslim. They both speak Javanese as their primary language. Edi also speaks English. Since Andi arrived in the United States 2 months ago before the interview, she did not speak English yet. Andi is 8 years old and has a younger sibling. She qualifies for free or reduced-price lunch. While Edi is a PhD student, the other parent is a homemaker and has a master's degree.

The third family is from Kazakhstan. Gulshat (mother), Aliya (older daughter), and Zhibek (younger daughter) identify as Asian, Kazakh, and Muslim. They speak Kazakh as their primary language and also use Russian at home. Additionally, they speak English. Aliya is 8 years old, and Zhibek is 6 years old. They qualify for free or reduced-price lunch. Gulshat is a master's student.

Data Collection Instruments

PhotoVoice was the data collection method of children and parents regarding their interactions with each other about civic engagement in different settings. Semi-structured interviews enabled children and their parents to tell their stories and showed their daily interactions about civic engagement.

Child-parent interviews.

Instead of individual interviews, I held one-on-one meetings once with each family to observe the interactions they would have as child and parent. The interviews took between 30 to 70 minutes. I used a combination of the PHOTO (Hussey, 2006) and SHOWeD (Wallerstein, 1987) prompts to guide the semi-structured interview process. PHOTO stands for: Describe your **P**icture. What is **H**appening in your picture? Why did you take a picture **O**f this? What does this **T**ell us about your life? How can this picture provide **O**pportunities for us to improve life? SHOWeD stands for: What do you **S**ee here? What is really **H**appening here? How does this relate to **O**ur lives? **W**hy does this situation, concern, or strength exist? What can we **D**o about it? I also added one more question: What kind of conversations did you have with your parent/child when you took this picture? Then, at the end of the interview, we went over the three guiding questions since families took pictures in response to these questions: (1) What does it mean to be a part of a community for me? (2) How can people make a difference in their community? (3) How do people in my family make a difference?

Findings

In this section, I talk about some of the major findings in detail under the "Finding Home Far Away from Home" theme and then explain affordances and challenges of PhotoVoice based on my experiences. I presented the quotes verbatim as much as possible with the accompanying photographs from the interviews so that the collaborators' voices could be heard accurately.

Finding Home Far Away From Home

The PhotoVoice project revealed that each family found a way to make this new place home for themselves and their families and at the same time stay connected with their lives in their home countries. During the interviews, each family mostly talked about their communities in the United States and also shared some stories about their lives back home in Indonesia and Kazakhstan. For example, Gulshat (mom, family 3) described the Kazakh community they have in the neighborhood, *"... there are lots of Kazakh people and it's also like a Kazakh community in [the neighborhood]. We all we like this [pointing at the picture]. We usually gathering together, celebrating some events with Kazakh people and had a lot of fun together."*

Andi (daughter, family 2) showed a picture of the wall in her new home in the United States, where she hung three photos of her and her friends, including her little brother. She said, *"this is my bestie in Indonesia"* and *"I'm missing them a bit."* When she showed a family picture, she said, *"I was so happy to be there because I can play with Nur* (pseudonym)*,"* who is her cousin. Similarly, her father showed a picture of him with his friends and said, *"They're meaningful to me, so it's about that shows gathering togetherness. When you're away somehow, it's just feels good to be among someone that you knew or you just knew."*

Image 1 *Andi with her friends in Indonesia*

Image 2 *Edi with his friends in the United States*

Aliya, Zhibek, and Gulshat (family 3) also mentioned several times their Kazakh community in the United States. After the siblings showed a picture of their friend group, I asked them:

> Betül (interviewer): So how did you become friends with these kids?
> Zhibek: Because they speak in Kazakhstan like us and they born there. And I don't know because they are besties [pointing at her mother].
> Betül: So they speak the same language with you and from the same country.
> Zhibek: Yeah. And my mom, like, likes her mom. They always talk together and they always share and they.
> Aliya: They was hug like [pretending to be her mom and her friend, everyone laughing].

Betül: So do you think when parents become friends, their kids also become friends?
Aliya & Zhibek: Yeah.
Gulshat: Thanks to us, you have like a you found your best friend. No?
Aliya: Yeah, I mean like.

Image 3 *Zhibek and Gulshat with their Kazakh friends in the neighborhood*

The connections that the parents have helped their children to have new friendships.

Another significant opportunity for new friendships was school. When I asked Birzhan (son, family 1) what he sees in the picture that shows the hallway of his school, he said:

Birzhan: Oh, I see Kazakhstan here. The flag. Yeah, the flag. I also see people here.
Moldir: Why do you think they put all the flags there in your school?
Birzhan: Because they wanted to know because we're a family cause like when we usually go to get breakfast, there's like people there that we are a family and like [the school] it says that and I think my school wanted to show that we're a family and from any country you are born, you're still, we're still a family.

Images 4 and 5 *Flags in Birzhan's school*

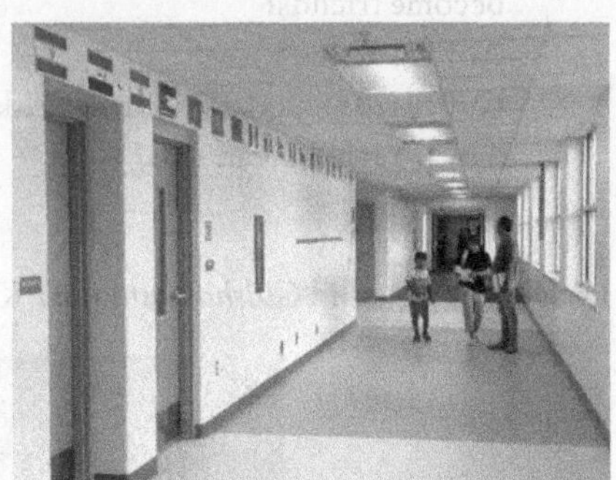

All families tried to make this new place home through making friends from their home countries. At the same time, they created friendships and bonded with people from different countries. For example, Gulshat described a picture of her daughters and their friends by saying *"Yeah, it's like a gathering of kids of all the students. It's like I was thinking about the diversity because all of them are like are from other countries and but they made a friend because of their parents."* A common point among the families was that in addition to their communities with people from their home countries, they also spend time with people from other countries with different immigration statuses in the United States.

Birzhan and Moldir (family 1) had a conversation about the differences between their home country (Kazakhstan) and the United States. Birzhan explained in detail the differences that he observed and experienced in two countries, especially in school settings. He said:

> I like America because you don't have to wear uniforms like in Kazakhstan and there's, for example, it's not like this [the chair] is soft. But in Kazakhstan, first of all, you have to sit like this, like sit straight and you have to like look at the teacher and when she comes, you have to stand up. And you can only sit down once, for example, like Birzhan you can sit down and you sit down, you have to sit down like this. You have to wear your uniform which is not comfortable. And when I try to run at recess I mean it wasn't comfortable for me to run but I can even go with my pajamas into American school.

Image 6: *Birzhan's school in the United States*

When both his mother and I asked him the reason for the fact that why the Kazakh schools buy wooden chairs instead of soft ones like in the United States, he said:

> Birzhan: Because Kazakhstan is a poor country.
> Moldir: It's again resources, right?
> Betül: What about uniforms? Why do you think children in Kazakhstan wear uniforms, but not children here?
> Birzhan: Because it's the real. I don't know why honest. I think why they make us wear these uniforms, because Kazakhstan is more stricter than America because the uniforms. I mean, they just want us to be. They just want us to be polite.
> Moldir: Yeah, disciplined.
> Birzhan: They want us discipline. And for example, Americans, American teachers, they don't really care ...
> Betül: I see. So you said teachers in Kazakhstan want students to be disciplined, so how about teachers in the U.S.? What do they want from students?
> Birzhan: They don't really care like. And they just care if you study good and if you so. I think why teachers are not strict, like in Kazakhstan is because USA is a kind country and.

> Moldir: Kind country
> Betül: Kind country. Okay.
> Birzhan: And whenever and my mom was talking about when, whenever, like in Kazakhstan people, people are like, they're like angry. They're like, look on the ground. But like US people, they like always smile like this. They're happy.
> Moldir: I think people are happy here. Sorry for interrupting.

This dialogue showed that Birzhan was able to make clear comparisons between two countries based on his experiences and involve higher-order thinking regarding the reasons behind these differences. It also revealed that he was happy being here and having this new home. Overall, although both the children and the parents sometimes felt homesick and had friend groups from their countries to feel at home, they built a new home for themselves here in the United States and even found some ways to bridge these two homes.

Affordances and Challenges of PhotoVoice With Families

Conducting a PhotoVoice project with families had some advantages and drawbacks. PhotoVoice method opened a window to children's lives. It enabled children to present their daily lives as they are and support them to share some moments that are meaningful to them. For example, Andi (daughter, family 2) said *"I choose the pictures where I'm in there and my siblings are there and my friends are there."* Similarly, Zhibek (younger daughter, family 3) said *"This is me. We are like riding bikes that time we were to the ice cream store."* PhotoVoice was a window to not only the children's lives but also the parents. Edi (father, family 2) said *"I didn't pay attention anything. I was just focusing on oh, this is a good thing to memorize, like a good event, situations that meaningful to revisit in the future maybe."* On the other hand, Moldir (mother, family 1) was very intentional about the pictures she took, and she had a story to tell based on them. She explained *"I think I was going to talk about I was trying to talk about man and woman work like work duties at home. So I took different things that like I am doing at home."* This project was a way to show her resistance to meet the expectations and her struggle within her different identities.

Furthermore, PhotoVoice revealed the aesthetic perception of families. Beauty in the picture was an aspect repeatedly mentioned by the participants.

For example, Birzhan (son, family 1) said *"There's a lot of colors in here. And it like whenever I look on that it like kind of makes me happy because I see all these bright colors,"* or Andi (daughter, family 2) said *"This is because they're beautiful."* As her father translated, Andi wanted *"to be able to copy, be inspired by the pictures."* He added *"I remember this because it's the time when we joined an art exhibition back in our country, so she took several pictures because she likes to copy."* These explanations showed that the children tended to take pictures of things that they liked or found beautiful. Similarly, Gulshat (mother, family 3) mentioned, *"I was thinking about that scenic view. It's like a very beautiful place I have ever visited and I was thinking about the nature and all of the community who are meeting in this place."*

Image 7 *Beauty from Andi's perspective*

Image 8 *Beauty from Gulshat's perspective*

Moreover, this project was a starting point for deep conversations between the parents and the children. For example, throughout the project, Birzhan and Moldir (family 1) had talked about differences in resources in the two summer camps that Birzhan (son) attended last summer. He wanted to show the gap in his pictures. However, he only had pictures from the school with more resources. Another topic that was discussed between them during the interview was gender roles. Moldir (mother) took pictures to show the responsibilities she has as a mother and Kazakh woman. She said:

> I was trying to by these pictures to raise awareness about complex life that mothers might have, especially international mothers, and studying and working and taking care of kids so that they are aware of that and I am educating my kids. From the childhood that there is no such a thing like a girl's responsibilities and boy's responsibilities. They should have like an equal amount of, you know, work done.

Images 9–12 *Life of an international graduate student mother from Moldir's perspective*

Moldir mentioned she does not have time to have deep conversations with her kids. She just realized they learn through observing their parents about some stereotypical roles, and it is time to start having conversations with them. She said:

> Moldir: He's learning but still the superficial knowledge of all of it. And I didn't take the time to speak about that until this study. So I hope he will get to learn more. And have less stereotypical, you know, things about, you know.
> Betül: Yeah, I'm glad that this project helped you to start this kind of conversation.
> Moldir: Yeah. And I feel like because of his answers, I see this so superficial and so, like, not deep. And I feel like, oh, I need to talk more about those social issues about, you know, roles of the woman I didn't even know that he thinks that I must do that.

This project was a starting point for them to talk about racial injustices (e.g., opportunity differences based on race) and gender roles.

PhotoVoice method had some drawbacks. For example, two families dropped out of my original sample due to children's limited knowledge about how to take pictures, not having time to take pictures, and unwillingness to take pictures.

Ensuring consistency of the collaborator data collection process throughout the project was one of the major challenges. In the original plan, both children and parents were guided to take photographs to help them answer the questions that I listed on the handout. However, in one of the families, only Gulshat, the mother, took pictures (on behalf of her daughters), which was mentioned by Aliya many times during the interview. When I asked how they decided to take these pictures, she repeatedly said, *"you [the mom] take them"* and *"I didn't decide [to take pictures], she decided though."* Gulshat preferred finding images online in response to the questions instead of taking pictures for her answers. Although Birzhan and Moldir took pictures, they were taken before the project, which means that the family used their prior images to answer the questions. Only Andi and Edi took timely pictures based on the questions. In other words, one family followed the directions during the PhotoVoice process. This situation seemed like a disadvantage at first since it made comparison across the three families difficult. However, it was actually an advantage of the PhotoVoice method because it provided families space to improvise based on their needs and preferences and make the process more personal and autonomous.

Conclusion

My intention in this study was to maximize children's agency to conduct their research while interacting with me and their parents as co-producers of research (Mayne & Howitt, 2015; Tatham-Fashanu, 2022). PhotoVoice method is promising for centering voices and experiences of people and especially doing humanizing research with children. In this chapter, I walked you through my project with international families that aimed to explore their understandings of community. Using photographs taken or chosen by families during the interviews supported them to tell the stories they wanted to elaborate on and enabled rich conversations with children and their parents. I finish the chapter with three recommendations on conducting PhotoVoice with families with young children:

1. Be flexible about the procedure because every family can have different circumstances. See variations as richness rather than limitations that show adaptability of the method.
2. Use tools (e.g., cellphones) that are most convenient for families. If possible, provide personal devices for children so that they can take ownership and be more intentional about their pictures.
3. Consider having focus group interviews with children and parents separately, which can create opportunities for even deeper conversations.

It is my hope that this chapter can provide practical steps and be beneficial to people who want to conduct PhotoVoice projects with children and their families.

The author would like to acknowledge Michigan State University's College of Education for funding and supporting this research.

I express my sincere gratitude to the families whose collaboration made this work possible. Big thanks to my advisor, Dr. Anne-Lise Halvorsen, for her endless support and guidance.

References

Adler, R., & Goggin, J. (2005). What do we mean by "civic engagement"? *Journal of Transformative Education, 3*(3), 236–253. https://doi.org/10.1177/1541344605276792

Alaca, B., Rocca, C., & Maggi, S. (2017). Understanding communities through the eyes and voices of children. *Early Child Development and Care, 187*(7), 1095–1113. https://doi.org/10.1080/03004430.2016.1155567

Breny, J. M., McMorrow, S. L. (2021). *Qualitative research methods: Vol. 59. Photovoice for social justice: Visual representation in action.* SAGE.

Bronfenbrenner, U., & Morris, P. (2006). The bioecological model of human development. In W. Damon & R. M. Lerner (Eds.), *Handbook of child psychology: Vol. 1. Theoretical models of human development* (6th ed., pp. 793–828). John Wiley & Sons, Inc.

Call-Cummings, M., Hauber-Özer, M., Byers, C., & Mancuso, G. P. (2019). The power of/in Photovoice. *International Journal of Research & Method in Education, 42*(4), 399–413. https://doi.org/10.1080/1743727X.2018.1492536

Derr, V., & Simons, J. (2020). A review of Photovoice applications in environment, sustainability, and conservation contexts: Is the method maintaining its emancipatory intents? *Environmental Education Research, 26*(3), 359–380. https://doi.org/10.1080/13504622.2019.1693511

Edwards, K. M., Herrington, R., Edwards, M., Banyard, V., Mullet, N., Hopfauf, S., Simon, B., & Waterman, E. A. (2022). Using intergenerational Photovoice to understand family strengths among Native American children and their caregivers. *Journal of Community Psychology, 50*(8), 3625–3639. https://doi.org/10.1002/jcop.22860

Fakhari, N., McIsaac, J. L. D., Feicht, R., Reddington, S., Brigham, S., Mandrona, A., McLean, C., Harkins, M. J., & Stirling Cameron, E. (2023). Looking through the lens: A Photovoice study examining access to services for newcomer children. *International Journal of Qualitative Studies on Health and Well-Being, 18*(1). https://doi.org/10.1080/17482631.2023.2255176

Gallego, G., Cardona, B., & Scholz, B. (2023). Using Photovoice to explore Bolivian children's experiences of COVID-19. *Health Promotion International, 38*(2), 1–11. https://doi.org/10.1093/heapro/daad033

Gilbert, B. L. (2023). Young children as artists: Photovoice in an early childhood classroom. *International Journal of Early Childhood Learning, 30*(2), 19–34. https://doi.org/10.18848/2327-7939/CGP/V30I02/19-34

Greco, V., Lambert, H. C., & Park, M. (2017). Being visible: Photovoice as assessment for children in a school-based psychiatric setting. *Scandinavian Journal of Occupational Therapy, 24*(3), 222–232. https://doi.org/10.1080/11038128.2016.1234642

Halvorsen, A. (2017). Children's learning and understanding in their social world. In A. M. Manfra, & Cheryl, M. B. (Eds.), *The Wiley Handbook of Social Studies Research* (385–413). https://doi.org/10.1002/9781118768747.ch17

Hauver, J. (2019). *Young children's civic mindedness: Democratic living and learning in an unequal world*. Routledge.

Herrick, I. R., Lawson, M. A., & Matewos, A. M. (2022). Through the eyes of a child: Exploring and engaging elementary students' climate conceptions through Photovoice. *Educational and Developmental Psychologist, 39*(1), 100–115. https://doi.org/10.1080/20590776.2021.2004862

Hussey, W. (2006). Slivers of the journey: The use of Photovoice and storytelling to examine female to male transsexuals' experience of health care access. *Journal of Homosexuality, 51*(1), 129–158. https://doi.org/10.1300/J082v51n01_07

Johnson, G. A. (2011). A child's right to participation: Photovoice as methodology for documenting the experiences of children living in Kenyan Orphanages. *Visual Anthropology Review, 27*(2), 141–161. https://doi.org/10.1111/j.1548-7458.2011.01098.x

Kiling, I. Y., Bunga, B. N., & Asikin, A. (2023). Photovoice study of parenting young children during pandemic. *Journal of Poverty*, 1–14. https://doi.org/10.1080/10875549.2023.2259891

Koh, S. S. (2010). National identity and young children: A comparative study of 4th and 5th graders in Singapore and the United States (Doctoral dissertation). Available from ProQuest Dissertations and Theses database. (UMI No. 3441687).

Mackenzie, S., & Talbott, A. (2018). Gender justice/gender through the eyes of children: A Photovoice project with elementary school gender expansive and LGBTQ-parented children and their allies. *Sex Education, 18*(6), 655–671. https://doi.org/10.1080/14681811.2018.1456915

Mayne, F., & Howitt, C. (2015). How far have we come in respecting young children in our research? A meta-analysis of reported early childhood research practice from 2009 to 2012. *Australasian Journal of Early Childhood, 40*(4), 30–38. https://doi.org/10.1177/183693911504000405

Oono, M., Nishida, Y., Kitamura, K., & Yamanaka, T. (2022). Injury prevention education for changing a school environment using Photovoice. *Health Promotion Practice, 23*(2), 296–304. https://doi.org/10.1177/15248399211054772

Raposo-Rivas, M., Sierra-Martínez, S., Alonso-Ferreiro, A., García-Fuentes, O., & Zabalza-Cerdeiriña, Mª. A. (2023). The rural school from child's point of view: A participatory research through Photovoice. *Participatory Educational Research, 10*(6), 208–228. http://dx.doi.org/10.17275/per.23.97.10.6

Samonova, E., Devine, D., & Luttrell, W. (2022). Under the mango tree: Photovoice with primary school children in rural Sierra Leone. *International Journal of Qualitative Methods,*

21, 1–12. https://doi.org/10.1177/16094069211053106

Shaw, P. A. (2021). Photo-elicitation and photo-voice: Using visual methodological tools to engage with younger children's voices about inclusion in education. *International Journal of Research and Method in Education, 44*(4), 337–351. https://doi.org/10.1080/17437 27X.2020.1755248

Swalwell, K., & Payne, K. A. (2019). Critical civic education for young children. *Multicultural Perspectives, 21*(2), 127-132. https://doi.org/10.1080/15210960.2019.1606641

Tan, Y., Pinder, D., Bayoumi, I., Carter, R., Cole, M., Jackson, L., Watson, A., Knox, B., Chan-Nguyen, S., Ford, M., Davison, C. M., Bartels, S. A., & Purkey, E. (2024). Family and community resilience: A Photovoice study. *International Journal for Equity in Health, 23*(1), 1–13. https://doi.org/10.1186/s12939-024-02142-2

Tatham-Fashanu, C. (2022). Enhancing participatory research with young children through comic-illustrated ethnographic field notes. *Qualitative Research, 23*(6), 1714–1736. https://doi.org/10.1177/14687941221110186

Volpe, C. R. (2019). Digital diaries: New uses of Photovoice in participatory research with young people. *Children's Geographies, 17*(3), 361–370. https://doi.org/10.1080/1473328 5.2018.1543852

Wallerstein, N. (1987). Empowerment education: Freire's ideas applied to youth. *Youth Policy, 9*, 11–15.

Wang, C., & Burris, M. A. (1997). Photovoice: Concept, methodology, and use for participatory needs assessment. *Health Education & Behavior, 24*(3), 369–387.

Chapter Ten

Capturing Divisions:
A PhotoVoice Exploration of the Impact of Political Division on a School District Community

Tabitha Dell'Angelo and Jodi Empol Schwartz

Introduction

THIS WORK IS an attempt to understand some of the dynamics in one large suburban school district in the northeastern United States. The district that is the focus of this study has been embroiled in 2 years of struggle that began with debates about masking during the pandemic and then evolved into disagreements about library policy, pronouns, and Pride flags. At the time of this study, this district had just passed the most restrictive library policy in their state. Some members of the community believe that extreme right-wing influences are attempting to use school boards to dismantle public education bit by bit. Other members of the same community believe they are saving children by shielding them from efforts to "groom" them into immoral adults.

The struggle that is highlighted in this paper is one example from many across the country. The district studied here has been embroiled in significant controversy in multiple areas. The tension that started during COVID-19 over masking continued even after schools reopened. Utilizing a photo elicitation method with community members, we see how the larger political context is parasitically embedding itself into the fabric of what were once healthy communities.

Perspectives.

Across the country, extreme parental groups showing up at school board meetings have become the norm (Wolfe, 2021; Talbot, 2021). ProPublica reported that a great deal of unrest at school board meetings corresponds with the time when school boards resumed in-person meetings in Spring 2021 (Carr & Waldron, 2023). In fact, Carr and Waldron (2023) report that 59 people were arrested or charged between May 2021 and November 2022. Prior to the pandemic, reports of violence at school board meetings were almost nonexistent.

COVID-19 changed the dynamic, making school board meetings highly divisive grounds that required police protection and presence at meetings (Talbot, 2021). What was once a division of conservatives versus progressives over the return to schools, and the role of masking, evolved into topics like critical race theory, sexual education, book bans, teacher conferences, indoctrination, and anti-LGBTQIA+ policies (Harris & Alter, 2022; Rizzo, 2023). Lengthy meetings lasting several hours filled with public comment from both sides have become the norm. Groups like Back to School PA, Moms for Liberty, and Woke PA (which have connections to the Three Percenters and The Proud), American Patriots Network, Free PA, and America First Legal have made their way into school districts throughout the state where this work was conducted. Several of these groups have ties and/or members who attended the attack on the U.S. Capitol on January 6, 2021 (Swenson, 2023).

Moms for Liberty, a 501(c)(4), is a far-right organization that engages in anti-student inclusion activities and self-identifies as part of the modern parental rights movement that has made its way into many states. The group grew out of opposition to public health regulations for COVID-19, opposes LGBTQIA+ and racially inclusive school curriculum, and has advocated book bans (Southern Poverty Law Center, 2024). Moms for Liberty champions "parental rights, has 26 [state] chapters in school districts, including 14 where individuals are actively engaged ... including one in each of the four ... collar counties" (Hanna, 2023). Pennsylvania's Bucks, Delaware, Chester, and Montgomery Counties, Philly's collar counties, are known for their racial, religious, and geographic diversity (WHHY, 2024). Due to their proximity to the city of Philadelphia, these four counties are known for their strong tax base for the Commonwealth. Once known for the state's bellwethers in presidential races and reliable sources of Republican votes, the four counties have been replaced with college-educated, well-off, and increasingly diverse suburbs that are becoming bluer and bluer with every passing election (Otterbein, 2020). Moms for Liberty have endorsed many of the candidates throughout this state and have been successful at getting candidates elected in school districts.

Out of this community engagement emerged parents who had not previously been politically active but were now energized by the desire to keep schools open and not require masks. However, while children were studying from home and parents were listening in, a new concern emerged. Some parents found the content that children were learning problematic—too progressive. These same parents were outraged that the human growth and development curriculum was being delivered to mixed-gender online classes. Little by little, public comment at school board meetings was not solely focused on masking and the health and safety plan. Now, parents started to show up talking about "grooming" and complaining about anti-racism and the teachers' "woke agenda" (Martin, 2021).

Book bans, culture wars, and calls for neutrality.

In the 1600s book bans were spurred by religious beliefs. In the 1800s a book could be targeted if it contained anti-slavery sentiment. *Uncle Tom's Cabin*, Harriet Beecher Stowe's novel set on exposing the hard truth about slavery, defied the pro-slavery sentiment of the mid-1800s. In the late 1800s, the target of book challenges was perceived indecency. Books considered indecent ranged from Walt Whitman's *Leaves of Grass* to *A Farewell to Arms* by Ernest Hemingway (Blackemore, 2022). Up until recently, sharing this type of history might elicit knowing responses about how much better off we are now. However, in the past 2 years many school libraries have been the targets of book banning efforts on similar grounds—religious beliefs, indecency, and anti-racism (American Library Association [ALA], 2024).

Efforts to censor and remove books is just one aspect of what is happening in many districts, including the focus district in this paper. For decades, public schools have moved toward more equitable and inclusive practices (Boroson, 2017). This has not happened quickly. Beginning in the Civil Rights Movement, historically marginalized groups began to challenge the policies and practices in public schools to achieve more equity. In the 1970s, these efforts resulted in beginning to close the achievement gap between students of color and white students. Resistance to these efforts in the 1980s undid much of that progress over the next few decades. Within the past decade there has been another concerted effort toward anti-racism, acceptance and inclusion of students who identify as LGBTQIA+, and overall diversity, equity, inclusion, and justice. Even while efforts and support for those efforts have ebbed and flowed, a community of scholars have continued to produce scholarship with the objective of promoting positive change.

Methodology

PhotoVoice as a methodology involves participants using photography to "visually document the issues that represent their communities, concerns and priorities" (Huber et al., 2023). Wang and Burris (1997) delineate three primary goals for employing this approach: 1. Examining community issues, strengths, and worries; 2. Fostering critical conversations through discourse; and 3. Advocating for societal transformation. Often, PhotoVoice is conducted with other methodologies. In this study, it was combined with a focus group interview that was conducted utilizing a visual thinking strategies [VTS] approach. VTS is a pedagogical approach where visual art is used to help students develop critical thinking and visual literacy skills (Hailey et al., 2015). The methodology relies on asking key questions and reflecting back responses to elicit more responses. The key questions are "What is going on in this picture?", "What more can we find?", and "What do you see that makes you say that?" The process is meant to encourage participants to become keen observers, justify their ideas, and develop a narrative for the image. This is essentially adding photo elicitation, the "simple idea of inserting a photograph into a research interview" (Harper, 2002, p. 13), to prompt thoughts, memories, and insights that may not be explicitly contained in the photographs (Collier & Collier, 1986). In this case, we inserted the photo into a focus group interview to allow the community members to hear one another and learn and build from each other's perspectives.

PhotoVoice With a Twist.

PhotoVoice is most often carried out with participants making their own images. Allowing participants complete control over the images used can be very powerful. That said, there are also ethical considerations. It is impossible to guarantee anonymity of people who appear in photographs and are particularly vulnerable to bias and self-censorship (Huber et al., 2023). With those ethical considerations in mind, we decided to give participants control of the photographs by allowing them to choose images that were meaningful to them and already published. There were many articles written and more than one photo essay about this community. Since those images were already part of the public record, it solved some of the potential ethical issues. Participants were asked to send in photos that were in the public record and resonated with their experiences with the school board. The three photos chosen for this study were each submitted by multiple community members.

Participant Sampling.

Participants were purposely sampled based on their level of engagement in the community. A call went out to 22 community members who routinely attend school board meetings, participate in messaging chats related to local issues, and have children in the school district. Participants who agreed to be part of the interview process were invited to a meeting to be held via Zoom. Of the 22 participants who were invited, 13 accepted the invitation. All participants identified themselves as women and were all between the ages of 40 and 55. One participant identified as queer, three were Jewish, and all had at least some college education. This subsample of the community is generally representative of the makeup of the community at large. It is also important to note that all participants knew each other before this interview.

Procedure.

After obtaining informed consent, participants were briefed on what was about to occur. It was explained that they would see a series of three images. After each image, they would be asked a series of questions. They were asked to refrain from talking over one another but instead to listen to one another and then add their thoughts. The order of the images was purposeful. The first image was one that centers community members, students in particular. I suspected that this photo would elicit a more positive response, encourage discussion, and relax participants.

The procedure for each photograph was the same. The photograph is displayed, and the participants are asked to take a full minute to allow their eyes to scan the image. The suggestion is to start from one corner of the image and scan back and forth, noticing as much as possible. This is important because the images are familiar, and they may perceive that they already know everything about it already. Prompting participants to slow down allows them to notice elements of the image they may have missed previously. After a minute, the interviewer asks, "What is going on in this picture?" As participants respond, the interviewer paraphrases and reflects back what is heard. It is important to allow for wait time to encourage participants' responses. Another prompt from the interviewer is, "What more can we find?" Again, the interviewer paraphrases to check for understanding. This provides participants with the opportunity to correct their understanding or add to their thoughts. This is a way to do real-time *member checking*. Member checking is a way to validate accuracy of data (Birt et al., 2016). The third question that is part of the interview is, "What do you see that makes you say that?"

Results and Analysis

In this section we will share each image and the ways in which the image was received and processed by the participants. Transcripts from the photo elicitation focus group were analyzed using inductive coding. Inductive coding requires letting go of preconceived ideas about the data and allowing themes to emerge from the data (Charmaz, 2008). Through the process of reading and interpreting the data, codes begin to emerge. Utilizing codes is a way to assign meaning to parts of the data to help represent the ideas, themes, and concepts (Chandra & Shang, 2019).

The themes that stood out in this focus group were signs, community, and protest. While there were three main themes, in this chapter we will focus on the theme of "signs"—both physical/objects and nonverbal cues. Peirce (1931-58) discusses the ways in which humans typically think in "signs." We both create and interpret signs to construct meaning in our world. He goes on to say that "nothing is a sign unless it is interpreted as a sign" (Peirce, 1931-58). As the theme of signs emerged over and over in the data, we found ourselves thinking about semiotics and how employing the study of symbolic communication might help in meaning making with these data (Hodge & Kress, 1988).

The framework used to categorize the theme of signs comes from de Saussure's (1983) two-part model of the sign. Saussure explains that signs are composed of two parts—a *signifier* and the *signified*. The *signifier* is the form that the sign takes. This can be the item, object, expression, or anything else that we "read." Each *signifier* has an associated *signified*. The *signified* is the idea, concept, or meaning being expressed by the *signifier*. From a semiotics perspective, both a *signifier* and *signified* are needed to form a sign. de Saussure (1983) also recognizes the subjectivity present in these interpretations. The relationship between a *signifier* and *signified* is constructed by the interpreter and can be changed. An example to illustrate the ways in which the relationship between signifier and signified can change as a function of context is the word "block." It was not that long ago that using the word "block" would indicate putting some kind of physical obstacle in the way to prevent someone or something from passing through. With the advent of social media, "block" might now refer to preventing someone from contacting you via an electronic medium. We bring this up to acknowledge the possibility of our own subjectivity in these analyses.

In the subsequent analysis, along with each photograph there will be a brief description of the discussion related to the image along with a table containing examples of words, phrases, and objects that were coded as *signs*. Then, there is an additional table that utilizes Saussure's two-part model of the sign to recode the data. In that table, it becomes clear that the use of semiotics changes what is considered a *signifier, signified,* and a *sign*.

Figure 10.1 *Image originally posted in a photo essay in the Bucks County Beacon*

The image in Figure 10.1 is from a photo essay (Crawford, 2023) published in a local newspaper. The subtitle of the photo essay read, "Students, teachers, and community members rose up Friday for the second protest in a week to voice opposition to the right-wing school board majority's Policy 321—which bans Pride flags and muzzles teachers." After asking participants to take a moment to take in the image, I asked, "What is going on in this picture?" The first response was "this is a protest." The theme of protest came up multiple times during the discussion around this photo. Another participant added, "... I see a student fighting for her freedom and her First Amendment rights." There were several responses that led me to follow up with the question, "What do you see that makes you say that?" I would typically ask that question if the respondent seemed to be making a judgment that was based on prior knowledge rather than noting something specific in the photo. This would force the respondent to take a closer look and identify, more objectively, the visual cues that supported their idea. Table 10.1 shows some examples of responses that were initially coded as signs. Table 10.2 shows examples of how participant responses were recoded using de Saussure's (1983) two-part model.

Table 10.1 *Examples of the code "signs" in Figure 10.1.*

Physical/objects	Nonverbal cues
• Pride flag • "...it's very well organized…the signs…the number of people…" • "...the signs don't look like they were rushed…there was thoughtfulness and time to produce them…" • "She has a prepared speech." • "...you have a child speaking and adults listening…"	• Showing love • people hugging in the background • "...it looks like a positive, joyful moment" • People are physically close to each other • "I see children and adults working together toward a common goal." • Colorful • "Visible allyship"

Table 10.2 *Signs from Figure 10.1 as constructed via Saussure's two-part model.*

Sign	Signifier	Signified
LGBTQIA+ support	Pride flag	Visual allyship
Organization/coordination	• "...it's very well organized…the signs…the number of people…" • "...the signs don't look like they were rushed…there was thoughtfulness and time to produce them…" • "She has a prepared speech."	This was a well-planned event
Respect	• "...you have a child speaking and adults listening…"	Children and adults working toward a common goal

Figure 10.2 *Image originally published in USA Today Network.*

Figure 10.2 is from a school board meeting where several community members were arguing in favor of a restrictive library policy. For some added context, after this meeting there was a report of one of the community members having a gun. After the participants had a moment to look over the photo, the very first comment was, "This photo is hard to look at, really hard, I'm sorry." One of the objects in this photo that was "signified" was the empty chair next to the woman holding the sign. The sign here was "danger." The form the signifier takes is the empty chair and the concept it represents [signified] is a gun. The man who was accused of having a gun had been sitting in that chair. This situation and this photo more broadly also highlight the salience of subjectivity. Only someone who was in the room that night would have that information and imbue the empty chair with that meaning.

Another example of how the bias of the participants was evident relates to the woman holding the placard. Depending on one's positionality she may be seen as a valued advocate or an enemy of free speech. A participant noted that the woman had "lots of documents in her hand ... and additional supporting documentation." Someone in the focus group noted that she had "produced" material. Some of the participants had been in the room the night this photo was taken. They had strong negative feelings about the message being conveyed in this image. Without the insider knowledge that some of the participants possessed, the interpretation of this image could have been very different.

Table 4.3 *Examples of the theme "signs" in Figure 10.2*

Physical/objects	Nonverbal cues
• "The woman holding the sign about child porn, looking at her face, has almost like a gotcha moment expression." • "Lots of documents in her hand, probably some prepared speech and additional supporting documentation." • Objects that indicate socioeconomic status (i.e., high-end bag, shoes) • Sign with "codes and regulations" • "Produced" material • "Far right ideological words of 'ban child porn', like those are very deliberate and specific" • Pillow – "someone prepared for a long meeting"	• Facial expressions – concern, anger • "Active listening" • "... a group of people actively listening to the speaker, and this one person who's clearly trying to draw the attention toward herself..." • "Paying attention" • "...some people are looking at their phones..." • "...I would assume this is some kind of meeting..." • Folded arms • Smiling • "She looks like she wants to fight..."

Table 4.4 *Signs from Figure 10.2 as constructed via Saussure's two-part model*

Sign	Signifier	Signified
Danger	Empty chair	A man with a gun was in the room
Far Right ideology	• Sign with "codes and regulations" • "Produced" material	"Far right ideological words of 'ban child porn'"
Socioeconomic status	Handbags, shoes	Higher socioeconomic status

Figure 10.3 *Image originally published in the Philadelphia Inquirer*

This last image was published along with an Op-Ed published by the school board majority. The opinion piece was titled, "We Voted to Ban Pride flags in Central Bucks Classrooms Because Students Should be Taught How to Think, Not What to Think" and was defending a policy that was coming up for a vote. This policy characterized someone's sexual orientation as a "partisan issue" and thus prohibited any visible symbols of support for the LGBTQIA+ community. The first comment after participants took a moment to view this photo was, "He's thinking – what did I do?" Some context that may help to understand this perspective is that although the superintendent of schools is typically seen as the person who is in charge, the school board has the power. In this case, as in many school boards, a nine-person panel—who may or may not have any knowledge of pedagogy, school finance, school law, and the like—are the boss of the superintendent. Superintendents are typically professionals with years of experience as teachers and administrators and many have doctoral level credentials in the field of education. This board was controlled by a 6–3 majority that was quite conservative politically and did not work in the field of education.

Table 10.5 *Examples of the theme "signs" in Figure 10.3*

Physical objects	Nonverbal cues
• Expensive laptops • Bottled water • Expensive haircut/color • Clothing, makeup, jewelry • "...contrast between the look on his face and his body language with the words right above him... effective communicators, citizens, collaborative..." • "...the two women standing kind of had a conquest..."	• "...[his] body positioning and the way he is looking down, and his shoulders..." • Gleeful expressions

Table 10.6 *Signs from Figure 10.3 as constructed via Saussure's two-part model*

Sign	Signifier	Signified
Submission	"...the two women standing kind of had a conquest..."	Not standing up for what one says they believe
Hypocrisy	"...contrast between the look on his face and his body language with the words right above him... effective communicators, citizens, collaborative..."	Hypocrisy
Socioeconomic status	• Expensive laptops • Bottled water • Expensive haircut/color • Clothing, makeup, jewelry	High socioeconomic status

Discussion

Community members in this study were highly engaged in issues related to the school board. Engagement took the form of attending and speaking at school board meetings, writing editorials for local papers, and working on election campaigns for local officials including school board elections. Participants chose images that were in the public domain that they felt were particularly meaningful in telling the story of what had been happening in their school district. Coming together to view and discuss the images provided nuanced insights into the complexities of navigating a politically charged environment within the context of education.

The findings of this study reveal a community deeply entrenched in political polarization, with distinct ideological factions permeating various aspects of school life. Through the lens of PhotoVoice, participants highlighted the palpable tension and divisiveness that manifested both in schools and in the surrounding neighborhoods. Images chosen by participants vividly depicted instances of ideological clashes, symbolic representations of political allegiances, and the subtle yet profound impact of political discourse on student well-being and academic engagement.

Moreover, the PhotoVoice project illuminated the disparate experiences and perspectives of various stakeholders within the school district community. While some participants expressed a sense of alienation and frustration stemming from perceived marginalization of their political beliefs, others emphasized the importance of fostering dialogue and understanding across ideological divides. Through the photo elicitation, focus group participants underscored the urgent need for cultivating empathy, tolerance, and civic discourse within educational spaces to mitigate the detrimental effects of political polarization on student learning and community cohesion.

Additionally, utilizing visual thinking strategies in the photo elicitation focus group provided a useful framework for participants to engage in discussion about each image. Participants listened to one another, shared their own insights, and expanded on each other's ideas. The discussion shed light on the profound and multifaceted impact of political division on a school district community, emphasizing the importance of fostering inclusive and empathetic listening amidst polarizing socio-political dynamics. By amplifying the voices and perspectives of community members through visual storytelling, this study underscores the transformative potential of participatory research methodologies in driving positive change within educational settings.

As school leaders, academics, and public intellectuals we need to be thoughtful and strategic about how to communicate our work and our stories. Kumashiro (2015, 2020) consistently calls on us to "name the moment." The idea of naming the moment asks us to be clear about where we are now and what got us to this point. Clarity in that regard helps us decide what our intervention might be. It is important to consider relationships between school districts and the community and how those relationships can create both opportunities and obstacles for addressing diversity, equity, and affirming communities for teaching and learning.

When we engage in scholarship it is always with the intent to add to the field and make a broader impact. When it comes to our impact on schools, it must be in the service of positive social change. Kumashiro calls for us to consider our interventions, as he specifically calls for a 360-degree view on this process. He calls us to consider the purpose of our scholarship—thinking about what it supports, what it resists, and what we hope to accomplish because of it.

The close look at how highly engaged community members are experiencing local politics may help to shed light on the divisions that seem to exist in communities across the country. A limitation of this work is that all the participants represented the same ideological perspective. Future research should include more participants who are representative of alternate points of view. It would be interesting to see if disparate groups identified the same signs when viewing the same images. We are still unsure if the right tact is to try to bring community members with deep divisions together or if it would be best to allow them separate space to make meaning of images. My inclination is that although the idea of bringing people together to listen and learn from one another is ideal, some communities are not ready for that yet. The level of distrust and animosity may impede the process. That said, Pratt (1991) writes about the use of safe houses as "social spaces where cultures meet, clash, and grapple with each other, often in contexts of highly asymmetrical relations of power." A courageous space for a divided community to come together and share and interpret images together could be a powerful next step in this research.

References

American Library Association reports record number of unique book titles challenged in 2023. (2024). American Library Association, March 14. https://www.ala.org/news/2024/03/american-library-association-reports-record-number-unique-book-titles

Birt, L., Scott, S., Cavers, D., Campbell, C., & Walter, F. (2016). Member checking: A tool to enhance trustworthiness or merely a nod to validation? *Qualitative Health Research, 26*(13), 1802–1811.

Blackemore, E. (2023). The history of book bans—and their changing targets—in the U.S. *National Geographic*. https://www.nationalgeographic.com/culture/article/history-of-book-bans-in-the-united-states

Boroson, B. (2017). *Inclusive education: Lessons from history. Educational Leadership, 74*(7).

Carr, N., & Waldron, L. (2023). *How school board meetings became flashpoints for anger and chaos across the country*. ProPublica

Chandra, Y., & Shang, L. (2019). Inductive coding. In: *Qualitative research using R: A systematic approach*. Springer. https://doi.org/10.1007/978-981-13-3170-1_8

Charmaz, K. (2008). Grounded theory as an emergent method. In S. N. Hesse-Biber and P. Leavy (Eds.), *Handbook of emergent methods* (pp. 155–172). Guilford Press.

Collier, J., & Collier, M. (1986). Photography in anthropology: A report on two experiments, *American Anthropologist, 59*, 843–859.

Crawford, K. (2023). Photo Essay: This Is What Resistance Looks Like in Central Bucks School District, Bucks County Beacon.

Hailey, D., Miller, A., & Yenawine, P. (2015). Understanding visual literacy: The visual thinking strategies approach. In D. Baylen & A. D'Alba (Eds.), *Essentials of teaching and integrating visual and media literacy*. Springer. https://doi.org/10.1007/978-3-319-05837-5_3

Hanna, M. (2023, January). Progressives are organizing to monitor PA. school boards in push-back to book bans, "harmful" actions. *The Philadelphia Inquirer. https://www.inquirer.com/education/souderton-education-voters-pa-school-board-watch-20230102.html*

Harper, D. (2002). Talking about pictures: A case for photo elicitation. *Visual Studies, 17*, 13–26.

Harris, E. A., & Alter, A. (2022). Why book ban efforts are spreading across the U.S. *New York Times*.

Hodge, R. & Kress, G. (1988). *Social semiotics*. Polity.

Huber, J., Bieling, C., Martín, M., Plieninger, T., & Torralba, M. (2023). Photovoice. *GAIA - Ecological Perspectives for Science and Society, 32*(4), 386–388.

Kumashiro, K. K. (2015). *Against common sense: Teaching and learning toward social justice* (3rd ed.). Routledge, Taylor & Francis Group.

Kumashiro, K. (2020). *Surrendered: Why progressives are losing the biggest battles in education*. Teachers College Press.

Martin, J. B. (2021). How a woke agenda infiltrated your local school board. *Washington Post*. https://www.washingtontimes.com/news/2021/oct/28/how-woke-agenda-infiltrated-your-local-school-boar/

Otterbein, H. (2020). A guide to Pennsylvania's political hot spots: The Keystone State has emerged as a virtual must-win for both Joe Biden and Donald Trump, Politico.

Peirce, C. S. (1931-58): *Collected writings* (8 Vols.). (Ed. C. Hartshorne, P. Weiss, & A. W. Burks). Harvard University Press.

Pratt, M. L. (1991). *Arts of the contact zone.* Profession '91. MLA.

Rizzo, E. (2023). This Pennsylvania school board made news for banning books. NPR.

de Saussure, F. ([1916] 1983). *Course in general linguistics* (trans. R. Harris). Duckworth.

Southern Poverty Law Center. (2024). Moms for Liberty. https://www.splcenter.org/fighting-hate/extremist-files/group/moms-liberty

Swenson, A. (2023). Far-right group Moms for Liberty reports more than $2 million in revenue in 2022. Associated Press.

Talbot, M. (2021). The increasingly wild world of school board meetings. *New Yorker.*

Wang, C. & Burris, M.A. (1997). Photovoice: Concept, methodology, and use for participatory needs assessment. *Health Education & Behavior.* Jun;24(3):369-87. doi: 10.1177/109019819702400309.

WHHY. (2024). What should we know about Philly's suburbs? In Montgomery, Bucks, Delaware, and Chester counties, what's going on you want WHYY to know about? PBS. https://whyy.org/what-do-you-wonder-about-phillys-suburbs-their-people-and-culture/

Wolfe, J. (2021, October 14). *Opinion: When parents scream at school board meetings, how can I teach their children?.* CNN. https://www.cnn.com/2021/10/14/opinions/parents-weaponize-school-board-meetings-wolfe/index.html

Afterword

By Dr. R. Mark Epps

Learning, remembering, and retelling the account of life honors both those who experienced it and those experiencing it.

Who are we?
Who knows us?
Who will remember us?

Education and technology have influenced how we frame, and answer, the narrative surrounding these three questions. Whether applied independently or together, education and technology allow us to examine historical artifacts, including stories, music, art, tools, documents, and language diffusion, each of which reveals glimpses of who we were and who we are. When melded into a synergistic process, such as PhotoVoice, education and technology allow educators and learners to break free from an enforced standardized examination and find alternative engagements that value individual learning, remembering, and retelling of our lives, our histories, from our experiences.

PhotoVoice, as discussed in this book, is more than a technology applied in education; it is a technology that encourages and actualizes learning and current information. In the preceding chapters, the authors' work showed PhotoVoice as a counter to both the legacy hierarchical education structures and the push–pull confines inherent in today's technological applications. Their work showed how PhotoVoice may be applied to divest from the business of teaching and studenting and enable educators and learners to forge new avenues in both educating and learning. In this positioning, this body of research on PhotoVoice in education provides a contemporary education–technology relationship that creates unique pathways for us to learn, remember, and retell life in our voices.

This collection of research shows how PhotoVoice may be leveraged to live and learn through co-experiential and participatory models, ones that closely represent how life *actually* unfolded and unfolds and that benefits educators, learners, and communities. The authors' work across education levels shows that PhotoVoice helps us answer how we arrived at this location and place in education, how we may partner with one another to achieve greater success, how we may engage learners where they are, and how we engage with each other in and out of the educational establishment. Their work also shows what discoveries may be found in and through the formal education and technology relationship.

PhotoVoice in education, in its realness, welcomes others in their time and their space. Separating from the traditional education constructs of sage-on-the-stage, scripted curriculum, and standardized assessments, including those found in postsecondary courses, PhotoVoice addresses critical needs in education and segments of life that many people around the world pursue—areas that reveal authentic and more representative experiences and outcomes for individuals and communities. While this body of work makes a positive contribution in education, perhaps its most important and lasting impact is that it honors both those who experienced life and those experiencing it. Here, PhotoVoice extends beyond education and into a place of individual and collective importance, a place that adds to the relational engagements of life and helps shape

who we are,

who knows us,

and who will remember us.

Editor and Contributor Biographies

Rebecca G. Harper is Professor of Literacy at Augusta University. Dr. Harper's research agenda focuses on writing and critical literacy and the ways in which authentic literacy can foster engagement, agency, and empathy in students. She may be reached at rharper7@augusta.edu.

Julia López-Robertson is Professor of Literacy and Teacher Education at the University of South Carolina. Dr. López-Robertson's research agenda focuses on advancing understandings about emerging bilingual/multilingual students and their families and on the transformation of teacher education to support equitable teaching for all children. She may be reached at LOPEZ-ROB@mailbox.sc.edu.

Carolyn (Carrie) Brennan
Western Washington University
Dr. Brennan's research interest is early childhood teacher preparation. She may be reached at brennac6@wwu.edu.

Tabitha Dell'Angelo
The College of New Jersey
Dr. Dell'Angelo is interested in arts-based methods, play, innovative pedagogy, and educational policy. She may be reached at dellango@tcnj.edu

Madina Djuraeva
University of Nebraska at Omaha
Dr. Djuraeva's research interests are multilingual learner education, teacher education, language policy, and translingualism. Dr. Djuraeva may be reached at mdjuraeva@unomaha.edu.

Jodi Empol-Schwartz
Montgomery County Community College
Dr. Empol-Schwartz is an Assistant Professor of Political Science. Her research interests are political science and American politics. Dr. Empol-Schwartz may be reached at jempol@mc3.edu.

R. Mark Epps
R. Mark Epps, EdD, is a secondary social studies educator in Georgia. He has presented on pedagogical, social sciences, and literacy topics at international, national, and regional conferences. His research interests include the political-education nexus relative to educator practices and policy development and implementation. He currently resides in Martinez, Georgia with his wife, Cyndy.

Jennifer Fike
University of Oklahoma; Oklahoma City Community College
Dr. Fike's research interests are equitable language ideologies and translingual writing pedagogy. She may be reached at jennifer.c.fike@occc.edu.

Kristen B. French
Western Washington University
Research Interests: Indigenous education, anti-Colonial teacher education, critical land-based family history, Siksikaitsitapi land-based learning. She may be reached at frenchk3@wwu.edu.

Elizabeth Astorga Gaxiola
Pima Community College and University of Arizona
Research Interests: community advocacy, activism, and the Borderlands. She may be reached at elizabethgaxiola22@gmail.com.

Emily Sein Yue Hui
University College London
Research Interests: environmental education, international education, comparative education, and global citizenship education. She may be reached at emilyhuiseinyue@gmail.com.

Meilan Jin
Western Washington University
Dr. Jin's research interests are cross-cultural study, play, teacher professional development, children's learning and development. She may be reached at jinm2@wwu.edu

Adilene Landa
Adilene Landa Garcia earned an Associate's degree in Arts and Sciences from Whatcom Community College. She earned her Bachelor's degree in Elementary Education with a major in Language, Literacy, and Cultural Studies and a minor in Education and Social Justice from Western Washington University. Adilene is a mentor, tutor, interpreter, and learner of life.

Vera Lee
Drexel University
Dr. Lee's research focuses on charter and public schools' engagement with families of English Language Learners; early literacy practices of multilingual parents and their children; and exploring civic education programs with youth in Germany. She may be reached at vjw25@drexel.edu

Dr. Rebekah J. List
Augusta University
Dr. List's research interests are multilingual learners, emergent literacy practices, and family engagement. She may be reached at bekahlist@gmail.com.

Dr. Sandy G. Mason
Prince George's County Public Schools
Research interest: As a Costa-Rican American and child of immigrants, Dr. Mason is a former teacher, assistant principal, principal, and instructional specialist in public schools whose interests include Latinx students, college and career readiness, family and community supports, language acquisition, immigration, and the needs of newcomers. Dr. Mason is the Hispanic Outreach Advisor for the Recruitment and Retention Office. She may be reached at sgeemason13@gmail.com.

Deborah D. Morbitt
The Ohio State University
Research Interests: the connections among student-lived experiences, schools, communities, and universities to support student learning. With a particular focus on social class, student and teacher identity, and critical whiteness she seeks to support preservice teachers' growth in becoming a teacher. She may be reached at morbitt.2@osu.edu.

Charlene Montaño Nolan
Western Washington University
Research Interests: Charlene's research explores how we can create conditions in early childhood that promote social and environmental justice. With a focus on preparing preservice and in-service educators to enact ethical change, Charlene's scholarship contributes to critical play-based and place-based, Indigenous land-based, and culturally thriving pedagogies. She may be reached at nolanc2@wwu.edu.

Aura Pérez-González
California State University Channel Islands
Dr. Pérez-González's research focuses on: (1) exploring the teacher preparation experiences of Latinx early educators to transform teacher preparation programs; (2) examining critical early childhood literacy practices that foster children's sense of justice, equity, diversity, and inclusion (JEDI). She maybe reached at aura.perez-gonzalez@csuci.edu.

Margarita G. Ruiz Guerrero
Western Washington University
Research Interest: As a woman of color, she has felt a strong desire and passion to advocate for social justice and equity in early childhood education. She believes this can be accomplished by creating spaces in which the inclusion of marginalized knowledges becomes an everyday part of learning communities, both in early childhood and teacher education. She may be reached at beruizgum@wwu.edu.

Laura Rychly
Augusta University
Laura Rychly earned her Ed.D. in Curriculum Studies at Georgia Southern University. She is an Associate Professor at Augusta University. Her research interests revolve around ways to improve life in classrooms for teachers and students. This has taken the form of theorizing about teacher and learner agency, accountability to classroom discourse, and improvisational theater in middle schools.

Betül Demiray Sandıraz
Michigan State University – Department of Teacher Education
Research Interests: social studies in early childhood, family engagement and literacy, humanizing research with children and families. She may be reached at demirayb@msu.edu.

Sally Wan Wai Yan
The Chinese University of Hong Kong
Research Interests: teacher education and development, curriculum and pedagogical design, and educational leadership. She may be reached at sallywywan@cuhk.edu.hk

Index

T

V

W